Art Galleries
to Visit in New Zealand

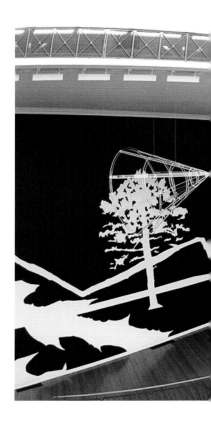

First published in 2011 by New Holland Publishers (NZ) Ltd
Auckland • Sydney • London • Cape Town

www.newhollandpublishers.co.nz

218 Lake Road, Northcote, Auckland 0627, New Zealand
Unit 1, 66 Gibbes Street, Chatswood, NSW 2067, Australia
86–88 Edgware Road, London W2 2EA, United Kingdom
80 McKenzie Street, Cape Town 8001, South Africa

ISBN: 978 1 86966 340 7

Publishing manager: Christine Thomson
Editor: Mia Yardley
Design: Trevor Newman

Front cover: Inspirit Studio & Gallery
Back cover (from top to bottom): The Diversion Gallery;
Aratoi–Wairarapa Museum of Art and History; Dunedin Public
Art Gallery; 4 Art Sake Gallery; Jonathan Grant Galleries; MONZA
(More Outstanding New Zealand Art); TSB Bank Wallace Arts Centre;
New Zealand Academy of Fine Arts.

National Library of New Zealand Cataloguing-in-Publication Data

Robinson, Denis, 1940-
Art galleries to visit in New Zealand : outstanding art collections
open to the public / by Denis Robinson and Gaye Ingold.
Includes index.
ISBN 978-1-86966-340-7
1. Art museums—New Zealand—Guidebooks.
2. Art—New Zealand--Guidebooks. I. Ingold, Gaye. II. Title.
708.993—dc 22

10 9 8 7 6 5 4 3 2 1

Colour reproduction by Pica Digital Pte Ltd, Singapore
Printed in China by Everbest Printing Co, on paper sourced from
sustainable forests.

Dunedin Public Art Gallery

Art Galleries
to Visit in New Zealand
Over 130 outstanding art collections open to the public

Denis Robinson and Gaye Ingold

NEW
HOLLAND

Contents

Introduction

This book is an attempt to provide a guide to the many art galleries of all types that are scattered throughout New Zealand. We were stimulated to write this guide when we recently heard of a visitor from Australia who commented, 'There seems to be an art gallery or artist's studio around every corner you turn in New Zealand – everybody seems so creative.'

The book is set out by regions, starting from Northland and moving southwards. We have included four classifications of art gallery, and they are as follows:

Public galleries (P) – those that are supported by central or local government or by local art charities, and which both exhibit and sell artworks, depending on policy.

Dealer galleries (D) – these are privately owned and operated commercial galleries which sell works on behalf of their selected artists.

Artist's galleries (A) – these are individual artist's studios or galleries that feature and sell their own works.

Sculpture gardens (S) – these are privately owned sculpture collections. Some sell work on behalf of their artists while others are simply private collections. Sculpture parks or gardens have been established in various parts of the country and provide access to some very interesting works, usually in amazing settings.

Most art galleries are generally free to enter and browse, but some may suggest a small fee or koha (donation). Many galleries, if requested, will provide a tour of the current exhibition and we have given an indication of this within their listing.

In general the public galleries have permanent collections of historical and significant works by notable New Zealand artists. Leading this group is Auckland Art Gallery and the Museum of New Zealand Te Papa Tongarewa in Wellington. But apart from the main city galleries there are others like the Eastern Southland Museum in Gore, the Aigantighe Art Museum in Timaru, the Govett-Brewster Art Gallery in New Plymouth and the Sarjeant Gallery in Whanganui, which have great collections, sometimes featuring particular artists or eras.

As our Australian visitor remarked, New Zealand does seem to have a remarkable concentration of artistic talent and endeavour. It has grown steadily through the country's short art history, merely 170 years since the first European settlers began arriving. With them came some very influential artists who adapted their styles to the clear light and strong colours of the new land. In the ensuing years the education system has put a high emphasis on the creative arts and this, coupled with the Kiwi propensity for international travel, has kept our artists aware of and involved with the latest trends in the art world. Add to this Maori rediscovering their own artistic heritage, particularly in wood and stone sculpture, together with the influence of Pacific colours and patterns brought here with immigrants from the Pacific Islands and Asia, and we now see works with an explosion of colour, vision and symbolism unique in the world.

In your travels through the galleries listed in this book you will see this great variety, as well as a lively mix of talent and techniques that should give you a fulfilling and exciting journey. The information in this book was current at the time of printing. However, as change is inevitable, please contact the publisher with any future updates.

Wallace Gallery Morrinsville

North Island

Northland

Art at Wharepuke (D)

Address: *190 Kerikeri Road, Kerikeri, Bay of Islands*
Phone number: *(09) 407 8933*
Website: *www.art-at-wharepuke.co.nz or www.art-in-newzealand.co.nz*
Gallery Directors: *Mark Graver and Tania Booth*

Building: *Purpose-built gallery space*
Opening times: *9 am to 5 pm daily.*
Admission charges: *Free*
Guided tours: *By appointment*
Wheelchair access: *Yes*
Toilets: *Yes*

Art at Wharepuke

Set within the award-winning, 4-acre Wharepuke Subtropical Garden on Kerikeri's Stone Store Hill, Art at Wharepuke is a purpose-built gallery space specialising in international fine art printmaking. The gallery complements the Wharepuke Print Studio, New Zealand's only dedicated non-toxic etching workshop, which was established by Master Printmaker Mark Graver in 2006. Mark is author of the handbook, *Non-Toxic Printmaking* (A&C Black, London, 2011) and winner of the 2010 Lessedra World Art Print Annual competition held in Sofia, Bulgaria. The gallery regularly holds printmaking exchange shows with international print studios and runs an open-submission printmaking competition, the Biannual

International Print Show. Although specialists in printmaking, the gallery also exhibits painting, ceramic, sculpture and video art.

Collection: Features award-winning works by Mark Graver and other established international printmakers.
Exhibition schedule: Monthly exhibitions, open-submission printmaking shows, international exchange projects.
Artists represented: Carsten Borck, Chris Pig, Clare Wardman, Dan Welden, Danielle Creenaune, Iain Robertson, Lothar Osterburg, Mark Graver, Nathaniel Stern, Sandy Sykes, Shany Shemesh, Stephen Mumberson.
Where to eat: At the award-winning restaurant on-site, Food at Wharepuke.
What else to do nearby: Take a course at Wharepuke Print Studio (non-toxic etching workshop, courses and materials); visit the historic Stone Store, Kemp House; explore the many walking tracks, the River Track leaves from Kerikeri Basin Reserve. On-site accommodation in self-contained eco cottages is also available at Wharepuke.

Parua Bay Gallery (D)

Address: 143 Te Rongo Road, Parua Bay, Whangarei
Phone number: (09) 436 5985
Website: www.paruabaygallery.co.nz
Gallery Director: Julie Nurse
Opening times: 10 am to 4.30 pm Wednesday to Sunday, and most public holidays.
Admission charges: Free
Guided tours: No
Wheelchair access: Yes
Toilets: Yes

This gallery is one of Northland's hidden gems. It is situated in a unique setting among the picturesque hills and beaches of Whangarei Heads, approximately 20 minutes from Whangarei Town Basin along the scenic drive to Ocean Beach. The gallery is host to an eclectic range of high quality original works, both modern and traditional, from throughout New Zealand. Work on display includes painting, glassware, pottery, jewellery and woodcarving, as well as stainless steel, copper and Oamaru stone sculptures.

Collection: The gallery does not have a permanent collection.
Exhibition schedule: The gallery does not have a regular exhibition schedule.
Artists represented: Richard Robinson, Colin Unkovich, Ingrid Boot, Mary McKay, Janet Bothner-By, Cathy Preston, Debbie Morgan, Carolyn Parry, Chris Van Doren, James Atutahi, Royda Vitasovich, Shona Firman, Keith Mahy, Rob McGregor, Michael Steinmetz, Ashley Hilton, Jan Cockell, Carol Robinson, Tanya Finlayson, Toni Dolan, Rochelle Goodrick, Jan Lorraine, Carole Prentice, Monique Endt.
Where to eat: Parua Bay Tavern is nearby for café and pub meals.
What else to do nearby: Play a round at The Pines Golf Club (18-hole golf course); make the most of the coast by going fishing, or enjoying a coastal walk.

Rawene Gallery (Te Whare Toi o Hokianga) (P)

Address: *2 Parnell Street, Rawene*
Phone number: *(09) 405 7899*
Website: *The gallery does not have a website.*
Gallery Director: *The Hokianga Arts Community*
Building: *Historic wooden building*
Opening times: *10 am to 4 pm daily (summer); 10 am to 4 pm Wednesday to*
Sunday (winter).
Admission charges: *Free*
Guided tours: *Friendly, knowledgeable staff are always willing to assist with enquiries.*
Wheelchair access: *Yes, ramp access.*
Toilets: *No*

The Rawene Gallery is located on the Hokianga Harbour in the historic township of Rawene. The gallery features work from local and visiting artists. There is a wide range of art including painting, sculpture, carving, weaving, photography, textile and jewellery. It supports the wider arts community in the Hokianga area, including the Applied Arts courses at NorthTec's Rawene campus.

Collection: The gallery does not have a permanent collection.
Exhibition schedule: November/December 2011 – NorthTec Graduate Exhibition.
Artists represented: The gallery represents artists from the Hokianga district.
Where to eat: Take in stunning views of the Hokianga Harbour from The Boatshed Café; enjoy fish and chips from Hokianga Takeaways.
What else to do nearby: Visit historic Clendon House; chat with some friendly locals; discuss the town's rich Maori and European history; or take a tour through the mangroves on the coastal boardwalk.

Reyburn House Art Gallery (P)

Address: *Reyburn House Lane, Town Basin, Whangarei*
Phone number: *(09) 438 3074*
Website: *www.reyburnhouse.co.nz*
Gallery Director: *Northland Society of Arts Incorporated*
Building: *A New Zealand Historic Places Trust Category II listed building, the villa was originally the home of a Scottish settler, Robert Reyburn Jnr, and is the oldest early*
settler house in Whangarei.
Opening times: *10 am to 4 pm Tuesday to Friday; 1 pm to 4 pm Saturday and Sunday. Closed Mondays.*
Admission charges: *Koha (donation)*
Guided tours: *Friendly, knowledgeable volunteers are always willing to assist with enquiries.*
Wheelchair access: *Yes*
Toilets: *Public toilets nearby*

The gallery is owned by the Northland Society of Arts and occupies a beautiful old pioneer villa (circa 1865–75). It is the only surviving building from Whangarei's early pioneer settlement on the banks of the Hatea River. The Northland Society of Arts has restored it to its present beauty with the interior being modified slightly to create a number of intimate spaces accented by dramatic wall colours. The grounds surrounding the villa reflect something of the 19th century with the cottage gardens containing many heritage roses and old-fashioned perennial plants. The wide lawns invite people to picnic and relax.

Collection: Works of prominent Northland artists dating from 1880, which includes some of New Zealand's foremost artists. Works from the collection are regularly rotated.
Exhibition schedule: Monthly
Artists represented: Northland Society of Arts members, travelling exhibitions, local art clubs, including patchworkers, camera club, cake decorators, dollmakers, woodturners and Northland art clubs.
Where to eat: Reva's On the Waterfront is famous for great pizza; try an old-fashioned lunch at Tiffany's Tea & Coffee Lounge (downstairs in the James Street Arcade); or drive out to Top Sail Restaurant (206 Beach Road, Onerahi).
What else to do nearby: Visit Whangarei Art Museum and Kiwi House Heritage Park (soon to be upgraded and renamed as Kiwi North), or Whangarei Native Bird Recovery Centre; explore one of the many beautiful local beaches.

Reyburn House Art Gallery   *Whangarei Art Museum*

Whangarei Art Museum (P)

Address: Lower Dent Street, Quayside,
Town Basin, Whangarei
Phone number: (09) 430 4240
Website: www.whangareiartmuseum.co.nz
Gallery Director: Scott Pothan
Opening times: 10 am to 4 pm Monday to
Friday; 12 pm to 4 pm Saturday and Sunday.

Admission charges: Koha (donation).
There is a charge for some national touring
exhibitions.
Guided tours: By appointment
Wheelchair access: Yes
Toilets : Yes

The Whangarei Art Museum is the public gallery of the district and the only public gallery in Northland. It is the permanent home of the city's art collection, which embraces both heritage and contemporary artwork. It is also the venue for national touring exhibitions and award-winning curated exhibitions, and is nationally recognised for the quality of its curatorship. The mission of the museum is to acknowledge, preserve and showcase the visual arts history of the region, with a focus on New Zealand's place in the Pacific and bicultural heritage.

Collection: This gallery has an extensive collection of heritage and modern works. Refer to the museum website for more information.

Exhibition schedule: Media releases, public programmes and films of the exhibitions are available online.

Artists represented: New Zealand artists of regional and national significance from the early colonial period to the present. All major New Zealand artists are represented.

Where to eat: There are many good cafés and restaurants nearby.

What else to do nearby: Check the time at Claphams National Clock Museum; wander through Cafler Park rose gardens, conservatory and fernery.

Auckland

Anna Miles Gallery (D)

Address: Suite 4J, 47 High Street, Auckland City
Phone number: (09) 377 4788
Website: www.annamilesgallery.com
Gallery Director: Anna Miles
Building: Canterbury Arcade (circa 1965–67) designed by influential award-winning, Canterbury-based architect Peter Beavan.

Opening times: 11 am to 5 pm Wednesday to Friday; 11 am to 4 pm Saturday, and by appointment.
Admission charges: Free
Guided tours: By appointment
Wheelchair access: Yes
Toilets: Yes

Anna Miles has a background as an art critic, curator and lecturer. Having decided it was more productive to be a champion than a critic, she opened her gallery in central Auckland in 2003. The gallery represents a select group of artists working within painting, photography, ceramics and jewellery. It has achieved a consistently high level of sales to museum and institutional collections.

Collection: Many of the artists represented by this gallery have work held in collections at Te Papa, Auckland Art Gallery, Dowse Art Museum, Christchurch Art Gallery and other private and public collections.
Exhibition schedule: The gallery holds regular exhibitions. Refer to website for schedules.
Artists represented: Edith Amituanai, Sandra Bushby, Kirstin Carlin, Kah Bee Chow, Octavia

Anna Miles Gallery

Cook, Darren Glass, Sarah Hillary, James Kirkwood, Allan McDonald, Kim Meek, Johanna Pegler, Kate Small, Richard Stratton, Isobel Thom, Barbara Tuck, Amber Wilson.
Where to eat: There are many choices for dining nearby but Sheinkin Café (3 Lorne Street) is well recommended.
What else to do nearby: Visit Auckland Art Gallery; relax in Albert Park; walk down to the waterfront Viaduct Harbour.

Art by the Sea Gallery (D)

Address: 30 King Edward Parade, Devonport
Phone number: (09) 445 6665
Website: www.artbythesea.co.nz
Gallery Directors: Mike Geers and Linda Geers
Opening times: 10 am to 5 pm Monday to
Saturday; 11 am to 4 pm Sunday.
Admission charges: Free
Guided tours: On request
Wheelchair access: Yes, on the lower floor.
Toilets: No

Art by the Sea Gallery is a bright, spacious art gallery overlooking the Waitemata Harbour in Devonport on Auckland's North Shore. The gallery exhibits original, authentic New Zealand fine art and represents over 60 artists. They have a large and varied selection of fine and contemporary art and crafts, including sculpture, ceramics, art glass, woodwork, etchings and prints, painting (oil and acrylic), designer jewellery, metal and 3D art, as well as contemporary Maori carving and sculpture. Primarily the artwork celebrates the uniqueness and diversity of this multicultural country and the people who live in it. It showcases emerging arts-and-crafts artists alongside established landscape, figurative and contemporary artists. A complete packaging and delivery service worldwide is available and all artwork is guaranteed 100% made in New Zealand.

Collection: A range of works by contemporary New Zealand artists.
Exhibition schedule: Generally exhibitions are held every 3 to 4 weeks throughout the year.
Artists represented: Brendan Adams, Andrew Bond, Robert Campion, Sean Crawford, Peter Collis, Rosemary Eagles, Bill Hayes, Paul Hooker, Raymond Jennings, Joe Kemp, Derek March, Garry Nash, Christian Nicolson, Kirsty Nixon, Rosemary Parcell, John Penman, Craig Platt, Daryl Price, Dean Raybould, Merv Sarson, Mary Taylor, Nicky Thompson, Jayne Thomas, Marc Vigor Brown, Ngahiwi Walker.
Where to eat: Platter, a café and restaurant, is next door.
What else to do nearby: Visit the navy museum at Torpedo Bay; walk the Devonport Heritage Trail; relax on Cheltenham Beach; enjoy the views and explore the historic military site, including tunnel system, at North Head.

Art by the Sea Gallery

Art of This World Gallery (D)

Address: *Shop 1, 1 Queens Parade, Devonport (opposite the Devonport Ferry wharf)*
Phone number: *(09) 446 0926*
Website: *www.artofthisworld.co.nz*
Gallery Director: *Angela Lush Randle*
Building: *Ground floor, Esplanade Apartments Building*

Opening times: *10 am to 5 pm daily.*
Admission charges: *Free*
Guided tours: *By appointment*
Wheelchair access: *Yes*
Toilets: *Public toilets nearby in the ferry building and the public library.*

This spacious gallery showcases a diverse range of New Zealand art – abstract, landscape, figurative, sculpture and wall art. They display a wide range of paintings and prints, as well as craft and object art from New Zealand-based artists. Informed, helpful and friendly staff can guide you through the gallery, or you are free to browse at your leisure. The comprehensive website catalogues the numerous works available. The gallery offers services in quality conservation framing, art consultancy, picture hanging, selection and installation services for corporate fit outs, as well as sourcing and facilitating artwork, especially commissioned pieces, from their extensive group of artists.

Collection: Paintings, photographs, original artists' prints, sculpture, glass, pottery, ceramics, jewellery, textiles, reproductions, craft.
Exhibition schedule: Refer to the website for an exhibition calendar.
Artists represented: James Lawrence, Peter Latham, Ian Hamlin, Christine Tizard, Fiona Whyte, Lynden Over, Tallulah Belle Lautrec-Nunes, Kelvin McMillan, Valerie Beale, Annie Smits Sandano, Stacey O'Neill, Timon Maxey, Lauryne Hart, Helena Blair, Clare Purser, Michael Rowland, Andrea Beech, Tony Roche, Vjekoslav Nemesh, Vivian Keenan, Wayne Sinclair, Robyn Barclay, Pennyrose Wiggins, Philip Beadle, Brian Gartside.
Where to eat: There is a wide choice of cafés and restaurants in Devonport.
What else to do nearby: The Navy Museum at Torpedo Bay is a great place to visit; there are many historical walks, including up Mt Victoria and North Head for stunning views; or you can always shop in the village boutiques or relax on the beach.

ARTIS Gallery (D)

Address: *280 Parnell Road, Parnell*
Phone number: *(09) 303 1090*
Website: *www.artisgallery.co.nz*
Gallery Director: *Jonathan Gooderham,*
Libby Storey (Manager)

Opening times: *10 am to 6 pm daily.*
Admission charges: *Free*
Guided tours: *No*
Wheelchair access: *Yes*
Toilets: *Yes*

A contemporary art gallery located in Parnell, ARTIS has been operating for 25 years. ARTIS has a strong exhibition focus and represents a diverse range of leading New Zealand and expatriate New Zealand painters, sculptors and photographers. It also incorporates a large sculpture gallery with an extensive selection of recent work by a current stable of artists.

Collection: Secondary market works by Milan Mrkusich, Don Peebles, Frances Hodgkins, Colin McCahon and Grahame Sydney.
Exhibition schedule: Monthly exhibition rotation
Artists represented: Sir Peter Siddell, Sylvia Siddell, Mervyn Williams, Pamela Wolfe, Ray Ching, John Blackburn, Pippa Blake, Marian Fountain, George Baloghy, Bridget Bidwill, Don Driver, Matthew Browne, John Edgar, Hamish Foote, Di Ffrench, Siavash Momeny, Warren Viscoe, Jim Wheeler, Carin Wilson, Michael Smither, John McLean, Roy Good, Gerda Leenards, Neil Miller, Mark Smith.
Where to eat: There are numerous restaurants and cafés in Parnell.
What else to do nearby: Shop in Parnell village; wander through the delightful Parnell Rose Gardens; visit Holy Trinity Cathedral and the Auckland War Memorial Museum.

ARTIS Gallery

Art Matakana (D)

Address: *9 Matakana Valley Road,*
Matakana, Warkworth
Phone number: *(09) 422 7818*
Website: *www.artmatakana.com*
Gallery Director: *Bronwyn Harris,*
Bronwyn Davies (Manager)
Building: *Opposite the Matakana Cinemas complex*

Opening times: *10 am to 4 pm daily.*
Admission charges: *Free*
Guided tours: *No*
Wheelchair access: *Limited, please*
phone for more information.
Toilets: *Public toilets nearby*

Art Matakana opened in August 2009 to an overwhelmingly positive response from the public. Owners Bronwyn and Bill Harris are well known in the area and have many years' experience, having established several galleries since the late 1980s. Situated in the heart of the popular Matakana village, Art Matakana represents a range of artists from young and emerging to well-known and established names in the art world. There are some sculptures and a few select pieces of ceramics and glass, but the emphasis is on painting with a wide range of media and styles. The diversity of works from abstract paintings to realist landscapes makes it possible to find something suitable for any home. Gallery parking is available down the right of way behind the building.

Collection: Refer to the gallery website for a collection list.
Exhibition schedule: Refer to the gallery website for current and future exhibitions.
Artists represented: Chris Meek, Candy Clarke, Megan Daniels, Belinda Wilson, Christian Nicholson, Dalene Meiring, Josephine Simon, Ande Barrett-Hegan, Peter Collis, Philip Kilmore, Hope Gibbons, Sue Willis, Kevin Passmore, Kirsty Nixon, Sarah McBeath, Sean Chen, Zeke Wolf, Tanya Blong, Ingrid Berzins, Jayne Thomas, Rebekah Dellar, Gary Nash, Denis Bourke, Rudy Van der Pol, Barbara O'Sullivan.
Where to eat: So many good options: Matakana Market Kitchen, Rusty Pelican Restaurant & Tavern, The Stables Restaurant and Blue Ice Cream Café.
What else to do nearby: Spend some time boutique and antique shopping, including Matakana Village Market (Saturday mornings); take a wine tour at Ascension Wine Estate. Refer to www.matakanacoast.com for more information.

'Matakana – Just up the road, but a world away'. The Matakana coast is a picturesque destination less than an hour's drive north of Auckland, which has undergone extensive growth and development in recent years. It offers quaint townships, beaches, orchards, market gardens, unique arts and crafts and exquisite wine and food. The Matakana coast spreads from Puhoi to Pakiri and offers a range of activities and experiences to suit all tastes. Experience the relaxed country ambience of historic Puhoi, Warkworth – with its serene riverside location on the Mahurangi River, or take a ferry from Sandspit to Kawau Island and visit the historic Mansion House. Morris & James Pottery, which is highly acclaimed for distinctive and vibrant glazes reflecting kiwiana and abstract designs, is also in the area and well worth a visit.

Auckland Art Gallery Toi o Tāmaki (P)

Address: *Cnr Wellesley and Kitchener Streets, Auckland*
Phone number: *(09) 379 1349 (24-hour information line)*
Website: *www.aucklandartgallery.govt.nz*
Gallery Director: *Chris Saines*
Building: *The main gallery was designed by Melbourne architects in French Château style and with an impressive clock tower. It opened in 1887 as Auckland City's Free Public Library and Municipal Offices. The part of the building devoted to the gallery opened a year later on 17 February 1888. By its centenary the art gallery had taken over the entire building, which was by now considerably enlarged, with the offices and the library having moved to new premises nearby. The NEW Gallery, across the road from the main building, opened in October 1995, due to the generosity of the Auckland Contemporary Art Trust. The building was originally designed as a telephone exchange and was extensively remodelled into contemporary art galleries.*
Opening times: *10 am to 5 pm daily. Closed Christmas Day.*
Admission charges: *Free, but charges for special exhibitions.*
Guided tours: *Free tours are available daily at 2 pm. Led by volunteer guides, these interactive 45-minute tours bring works of art alive for participants. Organised tours for groups are available by appointment. A charge applies.*
Wheelchair access: *Yes. All galleries and facilities are wheelchair accessible. Wheelchairs are available from the main desk free of charge.*
Toilets: *Yes, accessible throughout the gallery.*

Heralded in 1888 as 'the first permanent Art Gallery in the Dominion', Auckland Art Gallery Toi o Tāmaki remains the largest art institution in New Zealand, with a collection numbering over 15,000 works. The gallery has increasingly become a focal point of Auckland's rich and diverse cultural fabric, and now lies at the heart of the New Zealand art experience for both the local community and visitors alike. In 2011, the main gallery building reopened after a comprehensive heritage restoration and expansion project.

Collection: Auckland Art Gallery's collection includes major holdings of New Zealand historic, modern and contemporary art and outstanding works by Maori and Pacific Island artists, as well as international painting, sculpture and print collections ranging from 1376 to the present day. The gallery continues to actively acquire works across all collection areas. Acquisition funding comes from Auckland Council, as well as from a significant number of private donations. Works also enter the collection through gift, bequest or long loan. The Auckland Art Gallery supports the exhibition programmes of other public art galleries and museums throughout New Zealand and overseas by making its collection available for loan.
Exhibition schedule: Refer to the gallery website for current and future exhibitions.
Artists represented: The gallery's collection features artwork by more than 3000 artists from New Zealand, the Pacific and the rest of the world.
Where to eat: Reuben's Café on level 2 of the gallery.
What else to do nearby: Walk the Auckland Art Precinct – where in one block in the heart of the city, New Zealand's leading art galleries and specialist shops are working together to deliver Auckland's definitive art experience. Refer to www.artprecinct.co.nz for more information.

Bath Street Gallery (D)

Address: 43 Bath Street, Parnell
Phone number: (09) 377 5171
Website: www.bathstreetgallery.com
Gallery Director: Georgina Ralston,
Bridget McIntosh (Manager)
Opening times: 10 am to 5.30 pm Tuesday
to Friday; 11 am to 3 pm Saturday.
Admission charges: Free
Guided tours: Yes
Wheelchair access: Yes, at the rear of the gallery.
Toilets: Yes

Bath Street Gallery was established in 2003 with the aim of providing a contemporary exhibition space for both emerging and established artists. It has monthly exhibitions in which the artists have the opportunity to use the space as they wish, resulting in diverse and uniquely engaging gallery experiences.

Collection: The gallery does not have a permanent collection.
Exhibition schedule: The gallery has a regular exhibition schedule. See the gallery website for more information.
Artists represented: Harvey Benge, Grant Beran, Mark Braunias, Jo Bruce-Smith, Chiara Corbelletto, Geoff Dixon, Edwards + Johann, Anna Eggert, Jacqueline Fahey, Charlotte Fisher, Andrea Gardner, Peter Gibson-Smith, Robert Jahnke, Jee-young Kim, Robert McLeod, Kazu Nakagawa, Tanja Nola, Simon Ogden, Peter Panyoczki, Louise Purvis, Bronwyn Taylor, Katie Thomas, Riduan Tomkins (estate), Leon van den Eijkel, Denys Watkins.
Where to eat: Try Nori Japanese Restaurant, Non Solo Pizza and many more reputable cafés and restaurants in Parnell.
What else to do nearby: Visit Auckland War Memorial Museum and sculpture walk in the Auckland Domain; take in the harbour views at the Parnell Rose Gardens; check out other galleries nearby.

Bath Street Gallery

Brick Bay Sculpture Trail (S)

Address: *Arabella Lane, Snells Beach, Warkworth*
Phone number: *(09) 425 4690*
Website: *www.brickbaysculpture.co.nz*
Arts Manager: *Lisa Hannan*
Building: *Glass House, gateway to the Sculpture Trail, wine-tasting facility and café.*
Opening times: *10 am to 5 pm daily. Last trail entry at 4 pm. Occasionally closed for public holidays or private functions; refer to website for upcoming closures.*
Admission charges: *Adults $12, children $8, children under 5 free, students/seniors $10, family pass $35.*
Guided tours: *No*
Wheelchair access: *Yes, for the Glass House wine-tasting facility but no wheelchair access on the Sculpture Trail.*
Toilets: *Yes*

Brick Bay Sculpture Trail is located less than an hour north of Auckland on the Matakana coast. Created on the stunningly landscaped Brick Bay Farm alongside Brick Bay Vineyard, the Sculpture Trail is a remarkable outdoor gallery. The unique Glass House building, designed by renowned Auckland architect Noel Lane, is the gateway to the Brick Bay Sculpture Trail. Here you are invited to begin a journey exploring the very best of contemporary New Zealand sculpture carefully selected by a curatorial panel. It is a compelling outdoors gallery experience, where an ever-changing exhibition of around 45 sculptures by leading New Zealand artists are sensitively sited along the 2-kilometre trail. Sculptures are framed by towering native trees and majestic palms, abundant birdlife and green pastures overlooking the celebrated Brick Bay Vineyard. Smaller works are to be found in the shrunk courtyards, a perfect setting for their more intimate scale. All sculptures are for sale and change regularly as works are sold.

Collection: Brick Bay Sculpture Park does not have a permanent collection.
Exhibition schedule: The Park has a continually changing exhibition.
Artists represented: New Zealand's leading contemporary sculptors including: Graham Bennett, Judy Darragh, Neil Dawson, Paul Dibble, Brett Graham, Aiko Groot, Robert Jahnke, Virginia King, Gregor Kregar, Richard Mathieson, Dane Mitchell, Seung Yul Oh, Phil Price, Louise Purvis, Pauline Rhodes, Rachel Shearer, Terry Stringer, Tracey Tawhiao, Greer Twiss, Leon van den Eijkel, Rachel Walters, Richard Wedekind, Jim Wheeler.
Where to eat: Lunch platters, cheese boards, wine, tea, coffee and cold drinks are available on-site at the Glass House.
What else to do nearby: There are a variety of attractions nearby including farmers' markets, beautiful beaches, a boutique cinema, vineyards, horse riding and accommodation. Refer to www.matakanacoast.com for more information.

Connells Bay Sculpture Park (S)

Address: *Cowes Bay Road, Waiheke Island*
Phone number: *(09) 372 8957*
Website: *www.connellsbay.co.nz*
Gallery Directors: *Jo and John Gow*

Opening times: *By appointment only*
Admission charges: *Adults $30, children $15.*
Wheelchair access: *No*
Toilets: *Yes*

Connells Bay Sculpture Park is a 'gallery without walls'. It is a private sculpture park showcasing commissioned (site-specific) and purchased large-scale New Zealand sculpture. The park is only open by appointment. It is located at the eastern end of Waiheke, a 30-minute drive from the car and passenger ferry terminal. A two-bedroom guest cottage is available should you wish to explore the sculpture park at your leisure.

Collection: Graham Bennett, Chris Booth, Phil Dadson, Neil Dawson, Paul Dibble, Kon Dimopoulos, Fatu Feu'u, Regan Gentry, Christine Hellyar, Gregor Kregar, Virginia King, Barry Lett, David McCracken, Cathryn Monro, Peter Nicholls, Denis O'Connor, Julia Oram, Michael Parekowhai, Phil Price, Bob Stewart, Richard Thompson, Jeff Thomson.
Exhibition schedule: Connells Bay Sculpture Park is a permanent collection.
Artists represented: As listed in Collection above.
Where to eat: View East Winery, Passage Rock Wines café, Poderi Crisci, Cable Bay Vineyards.
What else to do nearby: Take a wine tour at one of Waiheke Island's numerous vineyards; explore the World War II military site at Stoney Batter Historic Reserve.

Ferner Galleries (D)

Address: *5/36 Sale Street, Victoria Quarter*
(behind Victoria Park Market), Auckland
Phone number: *0800 FERNER or (09) 337 637*
Website: *www.fernergalleries.co.nz*
Gallery Director: *Helene Phillips*

Opening times: *By appointment*
Admission charges: *Free*
Guided tours: *By appointment*
Wheelchair access: *Yes*
Toilets: *Yes*

Ferner Galleries has a long established reputation as an art dealer for more than 20 years, specialising in top quality works by major New Zealand artists. The gallery is located in the historic Victoria Quarter in central Auckland where a permanent display of artworks can be viewed by appointment.

Collection: Significant secondary-market works by Pat Hanly, Colin McCahon, Allen Maddox, Philip Trusttum, Juliet Peter, Frances Hodgkins, Edward Fristrom, Tony Fomison, Raymond McIntyre, Ralph Hotere and others.
Exhibition schedule: The gallery holds intermittent exhibitions.
Artists represented: Painting: Ian Scott, Steve Harris, Grant Hanna, Kura Te Waru Rewiri. Photography: Niki Hill. Sculpture: Greer Twiss, Marté Szirmay, Charlotte Fisher, Terry Stringer, Colin Webster Watson, Johnny Turner.

Where to eat: There is a selection of cafés and restaurants on Wellesley and Sale Streets.
What else to do nearby: Shop at Victoria Park Market; visit Viaduct Basin.

Flagstaff Gallery (D)

Address: 30 Victoria Road, Devonport
Phone number: (09) 445 1142
Website: www.flagstaff.co.nz
Gallery Director: Alka Fowler,
Ania Matuszczak (Gallery Manager)
Opening times: 10 am to 5 pm Monday to
Thursday; 10.30 am to 4.30 pm Friday to

Sunday. Closed Christmas Day, Boxing Day
and New Year's Day.
Admission charges: Free
Guided tours: Yes, if arranged in advance.
Wheelchair access: Yes
Toilets: Public toilets nearby

Flagstaff Gallery was established in Devonport in 1993 as the first dealer gallery on Auckland's North Shore. Now one of Auckland's leading dealers in contemporary New Zealand fine art, it occupies a spacious gallery both suitable for exhibiting and an enjoyable space for clients to browse. The gallery features custom-designed sliding racks with an expanded display capacity for more than 1000 artworks. The aim of the gallery is to provide a friendly, relaxed environment in which to make a wide variety of quality art accessible to all. Well-established and new artists contribute to their exhibition programme, which includes painting, sculpture and hand-worked prints. A range of services are available, including commissions, consultation, framing, wedding and gift registers, and shipping of purchases worldwide.

Collection: The gallery does not have a permanent collection.
Exhibition schedule: Refer to the gallery website for current and future exhibitions.
Artists represented: Approximately 70 New Zealand artists.
Where to eat: There are many cafés and restaurants in Devonport village, or you could order fish and chips to eat on Devonport Beach.
What else to do nearby: Explore Devonport village; walk up Mt Victoria for spectacular views of the Hauraki Gulf; enjoy the numerous sightseeing options in Devonport.

Gow Langsford Gallery (D)

Address: 26 Lorne Street, Auckland
Phone number: (09) 303 4290
Website: www.gowlangsfordgallery.com
Gallery Directors: Gary Langsford and
John Gow
Building: Gow Langsford is situated on the
ground floor of the former Lorne Street
Backpackers building, which was completely

refurbished in 2008.
Opening times: 10 am to 6 pm Monday to
Friday; 10 am to 4 pm Saturday.
Admission charges: Free
Guided tours: Yes, if arranged in advance.
Wheelchair access: Yes
Toilets: Yes

Gary Langsford and John Gow opened Gow Langsford Gallery in 1987. The gallery has developed into one of New Zealand's most influential dealer galleries, having hosted some 300 exhibitions over the past two decades. Gow Langsford is a commercial art space committed to fostering and promoting the best contemporary art from New Zealand and abroad. With a diverse stable of artists covering painting, sculpture, printmaking and photography, Gow Langsford Gallery represents established as well as early- to mid-career artists, so there is something to suit every collector. The gallery consistently strives to provide a forum through which its artists may be exposed to local, national and international audiences. This includes a regular and varied exhibition schedule as well as frequent participation at major international art events. As part of premier arts destination, Auckland Art Precinct, Gow Langsford is situated in a block of leading dealer and public galleries.

Gow Langsford Gallery

Collection: As well as representing contemporary local and international artists, the gallery also deals in works from the secondary market, including works by Colin McCahon, Ralph Hotere, Andy Warhol and Jeff Koons.

Exhibition schedule: The gallery's schedule of exhibitions combines solo and curated shows. Refer to the gallery website for current and future exhibitions.

Artists represented: Sara Hughes, Gregor Kregar, Max Gimblett, Judy Millar, Karl Maughan, Dick Frizzell, Dale Frank, Paul Dibble, Allen Maddox, David McCracken, Reuben Paterson, John Pule, Simon Ingram, James Cousins, Tony Cragg, Darryn George, Chris Heaphy, Antonio Murado and Bernar Venet.

Where to eat: There are many reputable cafés and restaurants on and around Lorne Street.

What else to do nearby: Walk the Auckland Art Precinct – where in one block in the heart of the city, New Zealand's leading art galleries and specialist shops are working together to deliver Auckland's definitive art experience. Refer to www.artprecinct.co.nz.

Gus Fisher Gallery (P)

Address: *74 Shortland Street, Auckland*
Phone number: *(09) 923 6646*
Website: *www.gusfishergallery.auckland.ac.nz*
Gallery Director: *Linda Tyler*
Building: *This historic landmark brick building played a crucial role in the development of radio and television in New Zealand. It was brought to life in 2000 as the Kenneth Myers Centre, the home of*

SCARPA, the University of Auckland's School of Creative and Performing Arts.
Opening times: *10 am to 5 pm Tuesday to Friday; 12 pm to 4 pm Saturday.*
Admission charges: *Free*
Guided tours: *On request*
Wheelchair access: *Yes*
Toilets: *Yes*

Situated in the historic Kenneth Myers Centre, which began life as the home of the broadcasting studios for radio station 1YA, Gus Fisher Gallery is the University of Auckland's art gallery. As such, it is committed to promoting the evolution of visual arts and culture. The gallery actively fosters creative and academic research, encourages curatorial practice and the development of postgraduate study in the visual arts, therefore making a valuable contribution to cultural heritage and museum studies, both at the university and in the wider community. Exhibitions of contemporary and historical art focus on New Zealand and the wider Pacific area, but also feature overseas work relevant to New Zealand. The gallery is also used for teaching and learning, performances, readings, talks and demonstrations.

Gus Fisher Gallery

Collection: The university's art collection began in 1966 with two works by Colin McCahon. It now comprises over 1600 works of sculpture, painting, drawing, ceramics, glass, fibre arts, photography and new media. Included are major works by Frances Hodgkins, Ralph Hotere, Don Binney and Charles F. Goldie, as well as contemporary masterpieces by sculptor Neil Dawson and neon work by Paul Hartigan. Distributed throughout the Grafton, city and Epsom campuses, the art collection has its home base at the Gus Fisher Gallery.

Exhibition schedule: The gallery holds exhibitions throughout the year with changing exhibitions every 6 to 8 weeks.

Artists represented: Those with an association to the University of Auckland including: Sara Hughes, Roger Mortimer, Andrew McLeod, Rohan Wealleans, Seung

Yul Oh, Jae Hoon Lee, Fiona Pardington, Megan Jenkinson, Michael Parekowhai, Ruth Watson, Reuben Paterson, Pat Hanly, Lisa Reihana, Daniel Waswas, Len Castle, Ann Robinson, Chiara Corbelletto, Charlotte Fisher, Denis O'Connor, Robert Jahnke, Peter Nicholls, Claudia Pond Eyley, Robin White, Selwyn Muru and Maurice Smith.

Where to eat: There is a wide selection of cafés and restaurants in Shortland Street, High Street, Durham Lane, Vulcan Lane and Queen Street.

What else to do nearby: Visit Voyager: New Zealand Maritime Museum; shop at the fashion boutiques on High Street and O'Connell Streets, or for secondhand books at Jason Books (O'Connell Street) and new books at Unity Books on High Street.

International Art Centre (D)

Address: *272 Parnell Road, Parnell*
Phone number: *(09) 379 4010 or 0800 800 322*
Website: *www.internationalartcentre.co.nz*
Gallery Directors: *Frances Davies and Richard Thomson*
Opening times: *9 am to 5.30 pm*

Monday to Friday; 10 am to 5 pm Saturday; 11 am to 4 pm Sunday.
Admission charges: *Free*
Guided tours: *No*
Wheelchair access: *Yes*
Toilets: *Yes*

The International Art Centre was Parnell's first gallery and has been at the forefront of the New Zealand art market since 1971. The combination of gallery and auction house affords an opportunity to view, acquire, sell and enjoy a wide selection of art. From historical works by artists such as Charles F. Goldie and Frances Hodgkins to contemporary Italian, Australian and New Zealand paintings, quality is the benchmark.

Collection: Refer to the gallery website for a collection list.
Exhibition schedule: See the gallery website or contact the gallery for current exhibition details.
Artists represented: Franco Anselmi, Anthony Blake, Paolo Canetti, Colette Cheyne, Paul Coney, Harold Coop, Brian Dahlberg, Gaston De Vel, Tracy Ellerton, Eugenea, Philip Holmes, Lawrence Leitch, Marietta, Carlo Mirabasso, Judith Moreton, Roger Morris, Darcy Nicholas, Mike Norris, Lance O'Gorman, Don Packwood, Patricia Payne, Raimondo Roberti, Eros Rumor, Kasey Sealy, Maria Serafina, Geoffrey Shaw, Ted Sherwen, Henryk Szydlowski, Bruce Treloar, James Watkins, Simon Williams.

Where to eat: Try Non Solo Pizza for lunch or dinner and Casa del Gelato for delicious treats.

What else to do nearby: Parnell is known for its charming boutiques, such as Graeme Thompson Antique Jewellery and Passion for Paper; visit Parnell Rose Gardens, the Holy Trinity Cathedral and Auckland War Memorial Museum.

International Art Centre

John Leech Gallery (D)

Address: *28 Wellesley Street (cnr Kitchener and Wellesley Streets), Auckland*
Phone number: *(09) 303 9395*
Website: *www.johnleechgallery.co.nz*
Gallery Directors: *John Gow and Gary Langsford*
Building: *The historic St James Building is a New Zealand Historic Places Category II listed building. Built in 1913 it has had several reincarnations over its lifetime, initially being the first YMCA in New Zealand. It has also* *been the offices for Auckland District Health and was converted into apartments in the late 1990s.*
Opening times: *10 am to 6 pm Monday to Friday; 10 am to 4 pm Saturday.*
Admission charges: *Free*
Guided tours: *On request*
Wheelchair access: *Yes*
Toilets: *Public toilets in the public library across the road.*

John Leech Gallery, established in 1855, is New Zealand's oldest dealer gallery. More than 150 years after its establishment, the gallery continues to specialise in the sale of historical works by some of New Zealand's most significant artists and to develop its commitment to contemporary artists in New Zealand. It has a fascinating history including its development from the birth of the gallery on High Street to where it sits on Wellesley Street today. However, it has always retained the name of its creator – John Leech. An interesting résumé on the life of the gallery can be read on the gallery website.

Collection: The collection includes work by contemporary artists as well as artefacts and work by Charles F. Goldie, Tene Waitere and L. J. Steele.
Exhibition schedule: Exhibitions are updated every 4 weeks.
Artists represented: Martin Ball, Richard McWhannell, Liam Barr, Justin Boroughs, Patrick Reynolds, Rodney Fumpston, Charlotte Graham, Peter James Smith, Lyonel Grant, Sofia Tekela-Smith, Michael Hight, John Walsh, Te Kaha.
Where to eat: There are numerous cafés and restaurants in the locality.
What else to do nearby: Walk the Auckland Art Precinct – where in one block in the heart of the city, New Zealand's leading art galleries and specialist shops are working together to deliver Auckland's definitive art experience. Refer to www.artprecinct.co.nz for more information.

Jonathan Grant Galleries (D)

Address: *280 Parnell Road, Parnell*
Phone number: *(09) 308 9125*
Website: *www.jgg.co.nz*
Gallery Director: *Jonathan Gooderham, Belinda May (Gallery Manager)*
Opening times: *9.30 am to 5.30 pm* *Monday to Friday; 10 am to 4 pm Saturday; 1 pm to 4 pm Sunday.*
Admission charges: *Free*
Guided tours: *No*
Wheelchair access: *Yes*
Toilets: *No*

Jonathan Grant Galleries

Jonathan Grant Galleries displays British and Continental 19th- and 20th-century paintings and important New Zealand 19th-century historical watercolours. The gallery has regular catalogue exhibitions, which include artists such as Frances Hodgkins, Charles F. Goldie, Sydney Lough Thompson, Charles Blomfield and Peter McIntyre.

Collection: Charles F. Goldie, Peter McIntyre, Frances Hodgkins.
Exhibition schedule: Monthly
Artists represented: J. Steven Dews, Shen Ming Cun, Ken Kendall, Piera McArthur, Ken Knight, Nick Cuthell, Lucille Cranwell, Peter O'Hagan, Paul Hanrahan, John Badcock.
Where to eat: There are excellent cafés and restaurants in Parnell Village.
What else to do nearby: Take in Auckland War Memorial Museum; visit Auckland City Art Gallery; or go in the other direction to admire the roses in the Parnell Rose Gardens.

Kaipara Coast Sculpture Gardens (S)

Address: 1481 Kaipara Coast Highway (SH16), Kaukapakapa
Phone number: (09) 420 5655 or 0800 420 5655
Website: www.sculpturegardens.co.nz
Gallery Director: David Bayly
Opening times: 9 am to 5 pm daily. Last admissions at 4 pm. Closed Christmas Day and the morning of Anzac Day.

Admission charges: Adults $10, children (5–13 years) $5, over 60s/students $9, groups over 10 $8 per person.
Guided tours: Available with the curator Sally Lush by appointment. Additional charges apply.
Wheelchair access: No
Toilets: Yes

Kaipara Coast Sculpture Gardens is a tranquil, peaceful oasis on a rural property just north of Kaukapakapa, a 40-minute drive from Auckland. It features 60 selected contemporary sculptures created by established and emerging New Zealand artists. Against the backdrop of the Kaipara Harbour, the 1-kilometre trail winds through a secluded valley containing a

Kaipara Coast Sculpture Gardens

slice of almost every type of iconic New Zealand landscape – manicured lawns, citrus orchards, grassy slopes, regenerating bush, old farm fences, pine forest, potagers and ponds. Sculpture, sound and installation works selected and developed for each context make mini-galleries within the valley. Works are revealed as the path twists and turns, sculptures are seen from vantage points where picnic spots and seating invite visitors to rest and contemplate the art.

The inspiration for the sculpture garden came from David Bayly, his aim being to create a place where visitors can stroll along a gentle trail and find inspiration for selecting sculptures and plants to enhance their gardens and property while enjoying great views. All the works are for sale and the sculptures on display change each year in November to give visitors a fresh experience on each visit.

Collection: 60 sculptures by contemporary New Zealand artists including works in steel, glass and ceramics.

Exhibition schedule: Annual exhibition changes each November.

Artists represented: Alex Stone, Ben Caldwell, Bruce Young, Cherrie James, Colleen Ryan-Priest, Daryl Fagence, David Poole, Diane McGarvey, Elaine Barry Conway, Gaye Jurisich, Gill Gatfield, Helen Pollock, Jonathan Bowman, Lauren Kitts, Linda Pringle, Margaret Sumich, Mark Hudson, Matthew Williams, Peter Lange, Phil Bonham, Raynor Dunn, Richard Sparke, Rose Petterson, Sally Lush, Sheree Edwards, Trish Clarke.

Where to eat: Ice creams, hot and cold drinks available on-site. The nearest café is at Kaukapakapa Hotel or DD's Country Café at Waitoki 10 kilometres away.

What else to do nearby: Visit the Estuary Arts Centre at Orewa Omeru Reserve; walk Mt Auckland Atuanui Walkway (½ day) or Atiu Creek Regional Park (½ day); play a round at the Helensville Golf Club; enjoy a harbour or fishing tour with Kaipara Harbour Cruises.

Kura Gallery (D)

Address: PWC Tower, 188 Quay Street (Lower Albert Street), Auckland
Phone number: (09) 302 1151
Website: www.kuragallery.co.nz
Gallery Director: Vicky Thomas
Building: PWC Tower

Opening times: 10 am to 6 pm Monday to Friday; 11 am to 4 pm Saturday and Sunday.
Admission charges: Free
Guided tours: On request
Wheelchair access: Yes
Toilets: Public toilets nearby

Established in 1998, Kura has highly visible art spaces for exhibition and retail in Auckland and Wellington, and represents a cross-section of artists from the renowned and established to the talented and emerging. Driven by a passion for supporting the growth of authentic Maori and New Zealand art and design, Kura provides a much-needed sense of what is truly unique to Aotearoa New Zealand by showcasing an extensive range of original, quality Maori and Pakeha art side by side. It stands out from the crowd for its bold approach to high calibre indigenous and New Zealand art. The gallery operates as a licensed stockist for 'Toi Iho', the mark of authenticity and quality for Maori arts and crafts and features traditional and contemporary Maori carving, original artworks, innovative design, unique jewellery, furniture and genuine pounamu (greenstone or jade).

Collection: The gallery does not have a permanent collection.
Exhibition schedule: Refer to the gallery website for current and future exhibitions.
Artists represented: Refer to the gallery website for a list of artists.
Where to eat: There are many high quality restaurants and cafés to be found in the downtown and Auckland Viaduct area.
What else to do nearby: Stroll around Viaduct Basin on the Auckland waterfront; take a sail on the Waitemata Harbour; shop at Downtown Shopping Centre.

Masterworks Gallery (D)

Address: 77 Ponsonby Road, Ponsonby
Phone number: (09) 378 1256
Website: www.masterworksgallery.com
Gallery Director: Eloise Kitson
Opening times: 10 am to 5.30 pm Monday
to Friday; 10 am to 4 pm Saturday.
Admission charges: Free
Guided tours: On request
Wheelchair access: Yes
Toilets: No

Established 25 years ago, Masterworks Gallery specialises in the exhibition and sale of New Zealand and Australian contemporary applied art with a strong focus on glass, ceramics and jewellery. It represents a select group of artists, many of whom exhibit and teach internationally, with the major emphasis on promoting the richness and diversity of craft and contemporary sculpture, particularly those that reflect the regional influences of Australasia. The gallery presents 11 exhibitions a year, with a mix of solo and curated group shows across three programmes. It has a strong international client base and offers advice on valuation and collection.

Collection: Glass, ceramics, jewellery, wood, stone and mixed media works.
Exhibition schedule: Monthly exhibition programmes of solo artist shows and curated group shows. The Jewellery Box showcases new work by contemporary jewellers and the THINKspace is a new educational project-based area of the gallery.
Artists represented: Galia Amsel, Emma Camden, Bronwynne Cornish, Kate Fitzharris, Jeff Mincham, Chester Nealie, Richard Parker, Ann Robinson, Christine Thacker, Lisa Walker, Stephen Bradbourne, Christine Cathie, Benjamin Edols and Kathy Elliott, Matthew McIntyre-Wilson, David Murray, John Parker, Hana Rakena, Katherine Smyth, Ann Verdcourt, John Roy, Paul Maseyk, Mike Crawford, Vicki Fanning. Refer to the gallery website for a full list of artists.
Where to eat: There are numerous good cafés and restaurants along Ponsonby Road.
What else to do nearby: There is a wide variety of boutique shopping along Ponsonby Road.

Matakana Gallery & Design (D)

Address: *Matakana Country Park,*
1151 Leigh Road, Matakana
Phone number: *(09) 422 9790*
Website: *www.matakanaartgallery.com*
Gallery Director: *Bronwyn Harris*
Building: *Matakana Country Park complex*
Opening times: *10 am to 4 pm Wednesday*
to Sunday.
Admission charges: *Free*
Guided tours: *No*
Wheelchair access: *Limited, please phone for*
more information.
Toilets: *Yes, within Matakana Country Park*
complex.

This gallery is in the picturesque Matakana Country Park complex in a real country setting with convenient entrances from Leigh Road and Omaha Flats Road. It is a large gallery space ranging over two floors and features some of New Zealand's most popular contemporary artists using varying mediums – painting, sculpture, jewellery, glass, ceramics, photography and mixed media. Great staging in the spacious gallery allows you to really appreciate the collection of works on display.

Collection: Refer to the gallery website for a collection list.
Exhibition schedule: Refer to the gallery website for current and future exhibitions.
Artists represented: Tracy Mathewson, Mandy Emerson, Shane Dudley, James Lawrence, Graham Downs, Grant Reed, Daniella Hulme, Amber Emm, James Wright, Tui Hobson, Lauren Kitts, John Ecuyer, Renee Boyd, Delwyn Ward, Gail Challenger, Justin Culina, Mark Dimock, Penny Otto, Jane Pierce, Matt Payne, Grant Marshall, Russell Jackson, Bee Doughty-Pratt, Helena Blair, Murray Stuart.
Where to eat: Enjoy a coffee at Country Kitchen Café or a meal at The Stables Restaurant and Bar, both in the park complex.
What else to do nearby: Visit Omaha Beach, Goat Island Marine Reserve (with glass-bottom boat trips) and Tawharanui Regional Park; take a wine tour at a nearby vineyard; explore Matakana village; be impressed at Morris & James Pottery. Refer www.matakancoast.com for more information.

Monterey Art Gallery (D)

Address: *5 Cook Street, Howick*
Phone number: *(09) 532 9022*
Website: *www.montereyartgallery.co.nz*
Gallery Director: *Sandy Starr*
Opening times: *9.30 am to 5 pm Monday*
to Friday; 10 am to 3 pm Saturday.
Admission charges: *Free*
Guided tours: *Gallery staff are available to*
provide assistance at any time.
Wheelchair access: *Yes*
Toilets: *Public toilets nearby in Howick village.*

Monterey Art Gallery nestled in Howick village offers a unique opportunity to access a variety of works from a diverse range of contemporary New Zealand artists. The gallery offers a broad spectrum of quality painting, ceramics, sculpture, glass, photography and jewellery.

Exhibitions are held regularly and the website is updated weekly to enable valued customers to be informed through a client database. Sandy Starr is the owner of Monterey Art Gallery and as an interior designer has a reputation for presenting only the very highest standard of work. Art on display in the gallery is only a small portion of pieces available; the storeroom is always full.

Collection: The gallery does not have a permanent collection.
Exhibition schedule: The gallery has a regular exhibition schedule. Refer to the gallery website for current and future exhibitions.
Artists represented: Dalene Meiring, Graham Young, Suzanne Wiggins, Darryl Fagence, Tom Folwell, Crispin Korschen, Kirsty Nixon, Evelyn Dunstan, Amber Emm, Cheryl Oliver, Sirpa Alalaakkola, Katie Gold, Jill Perrott, Peter Hall, Justin Culina, Garry Nash, Peter Collis, Leila Ataya, Helena Blair, Desiree Oosthuysen-Loe, Graham Ambrose, Clare Reilly, Heather Leonard, Merv Sarson, Megan Daniels.
Where to eat: Howick village is filled with a selection of eateries including Basalt, The Antiques Store, Coffee and Tea Lovers.
What else to do nearby: Every Saturday from 8.30 am Howick holds a boutique farmers' market with fresh fish, flowers, chocolates, cheeses, breads, produce and handcrafts available. There are also a number of antique shops within the village.

NKB Gallery (D)

Address: *455 Mt Eden Road, Mt Eden*
Phone number: *(09) 623 1464*
Website: *www.nkbgallery.co.nz*
Gallery Director: *Ngaire Beckman,*
Paul Hays (Manager)
Opening times: *10 am to 6 pm Tuesday to*
Friday; 10 am to 4 pm Monday and Saturday.
Admission charges: *Free*
Guided tours: *The gallery manager is*
available to provide assistance at any time.
Wheelchair access: *Yes*
Toilets: *Yes*

NKB Gallery is a contemporary fine art gallery in the heart of Mt Eden village. Mt Eden is a unique community that claims many prominent New Zealand artists as long-time residents. Because of this it is only natural that a gallery would exist in such a setting. NKB Gallery is committed to making the art of prominent and established artists accessible to the public, as well as helping to establish emerging artists. Each year the gallery holds a variety of exciting exhibitions, including solo, joint, group and stock shows. In addition to pieces displayed on the walls of the gallery, there is a wide variety of works in the stockroom. Some of these works will be familiar and some come directly from the artists' studios. The gallery invites visitors to attend the exhibitions and take the time to peruse the selection of works in their ever-changing stockroom.

Collection: Jenny Dolezel – *Intermission (1)*; Michael Smither – *Clouds 'I'm Coming Henry'*; Marté Szirmay – *Wish Fulfilling Tree, Winter*; Joy Chang – *Little Jewels*; Sylvia Siddell – *Feeling the Heat*; Russell Jackson; Ruth Cole.

Exhibition schedule: Refer to the gallery website for current and future exhibitions.
Artists represented: Lindsey Baker, George Baloghy, Stephen Bradbourne, Glenys
Brookbanks, Marcus Capes, Joy Chang, Anton Chapman, Ruth Cole, Anna Crawley, Luise
Fong, Peter Gibson-Smith, Russell Hollings, Russell Jackson, Samantha Lissette, Kate Jones
Madill, Rebecca Meyer, Anna Perry, Hanno Rol, Mike Rowland, Sylvia Siddell, Katherine
Simpson, Michael Smither, Marté Szirmay, Paul Woodruffe, Jan Young.
Where to eat: Mt Eden is well known for its cafés and restaurants, such as Circus Circus, De
Post Belgian Beer and Haru No Yume Japanese Restaurant.
What else to do nearby: Visit Mt Eden summit by walking or driving for exceptional 360-
degree views over Auckland; eat and drink at one of the many cafés, restaurants or bars;
shop for books, art or homewares.

Objectspace (D)

Address: 8 Ponsonby Road, Ponsonby
Phone number: (09) 376 6216
Website: www.objectspace.org.nz
Gallery Director: Philip Clarke
Opening times: 10 am to 5 pm Monday to Saturday.

Admission charges: Free
Guided tours: No
Wheelchair access: Yes
Toilets: Yes

Objectspace is a dedicated and award-winning centre for innovative craft and design.
Objectspace connects innovative objects and makers with audiences in order to expand the
cultural, economic and social options for object-making.

Collection: The gallery does not have a permanent collection.
Exhibition schedule: Refer to the gallery website for current and future exhibitions.
Artists represented: There are no artists represented by this gallery.
Where to eat: There are numerous cafés and restaurants along Ponsonby Road.
What else to do nearby: Recognised as a creative centre of Auckland, there are a number of
interesting galleries in the Ponsonby and Karangahape Road area to visit.

Objectspace   *Of Hand & Heart*

Of Hand & Heart (D)

Address: *3 Neville Street, Warkworth*
Phone number: *(09) 425 8855*
Website: *Under construction*
Gallery Directors: *Rick Urban and Mio Endo*
Opening times: *10 am to 5 pm Monday to*

Saturday; 1 pm to 5 pm Sunday.
Admission charges: *Free*
Guided tours: *No*
Wheelchair access: *Yes*
Toilets: *No*

This is a new gallery that allows you to experience visual and tactile treats wherever you look. American potter Rick Urban and Japanese artist Mio Endo have brought together the work of painters and artists from around New Zealand. Also on display is an extensive selection of pottery and ceramic pieces collected from over 50 New Zealand, American, Japanese and Australian clay artists. Mio Endo has assembled a selection of silk dresses from American designers, as well as accessories, jewellery and fibre arts created by various artists. Of Hand & Heart offers the visitor an unusually beautiful display of artful pieces.

Collection: The gallery does not have a permanent collection.
Exhibition schedule: The gallery holds shows two to three times a year.
Artists represented: Peter Collis, Peter and Jeanette Shearer, Cheryl Oliver, Greg Barron, Wilma Jennings, Kim Morgan, Ross Mitchell Anyon, Graham Ambrose, Tallulah Belle Lautrec-Nunes, Hana Ott, Margaret Bell, de Flute Glass, Fern Flat Pottery, Craig Fletcher, Nick Fedaeff, Jeff Thomson, Ron Hall, Fiona Tunnicliffe, Sang Sool Shim and Keum Sun Lee, Andrew Van Der Putten, Robert Rapson, Jack Troy, Warren MacKenzie, Rae West, Liz Turnbull.
Where to eat: Try Flavour Café next door to gallery, a selection of others available in the village or drive 10 minutes to the Ascension Wine Estate, Matakana.
What else to do nearby: Visit the craft cooperative next door and explore the charming village of Warkworth sitting alongside the Mahurangi River. Refer www.matakancoast.com for more information.

Papakura Art Gallery (P)

Address: *10 Averill Street, Papakura*
Phone number: *(09) 297 7510*
Website: *www.papakuraarts.co.nz*
Gallery Manager: *Tracey Williams*
Building: *Refurbished fire station*
Opening times: *9 am to 5 pm Monday to*

Friday; 10 am to 2 pm Saturday.
Admission charges: *Free*
Guided tours: *By appointment*
Wheelchair access: *Yes*
Toilets: *Yes*

Papakura Art Gallery is a small contemporary art space administered by the Auckland Council. Its operational mandate is to provide a balanced programme of quality exhibitions, projects and programmes that will expose the community to outstanding arts and artists to engage and enrich local culture and support community development.

Collection: The gallery does not have a permanent collection.
Exhibition schedule: Exhibitions are held every 4 to 6 weeks and the gallery is closed for 1 week between shows.
Artists represented: Papakura Art Gallery does not represent any individual artists.
Where to eat: Stop at Mottletop Espresso Bar (293 Great South Road) for coffee and fresh bread.
What else to do nearby: Visit the Hawkins Theatre, the Papakura Museum; plan a walk through Kirks Bush Scenic Reserve or a hike in the Hunua Ranges Regional Park.

Parnell Gallery (D)

Address: 263 Parnell Road, Parnell
Phone number: (09) 377 3133
Website: www.parnellgallery.co.nz
Gallery Director: Sally Souness
Building: Two-storey villa
Opening times: 9.30 am to 5.30 pm Monday
to Friday; 10 am to 4 pm Saturday;
11 am to 4 pm Sunday.
Admission charges: Free
Guided tours: On request
Wheelchair access: No
Toilets: No

Parnell Gallery was established by Sally Souness 35 years ago. It is one of New Zealand's leading contemporary art galleries. Situated in a traditional Auckland villa in the heart of Parnell, this gallery specialises in contemporary New Zealand painting, limited-edition prints, sculpture and framing services. Monthly exhibitions by renowned New Zealand artists are held in the upstairs area. On the street level there is a permanent display of paintings, bronze sculptures and original limited edition prints. The Parnell Gallery is positioned in the marketplace as being accessible to the majority of art buyers and art lovers. It is an environment where people can feel comfortable browsing and talking about art and artists in general.

Collection: The gallery does not have a permanent collection.
Exhibition schedule: Refer to the gallery website for current and future exhibitions.
Artists represented: Michelle Bellamy, Neil Driver, Michelle Farrell, Fatu Feu'u, Jason Hicks, Ron Hall, Otis Frizzell, Matt Gauldie, Stephen Howard, Russell Jackson, Sofia Minson, Dalene Meiring, Brad Novak, Tony Ogle, Helen Ollivier, Jill Perrott, Sue Schaare, Annie Smits Sandano, Vicky Savage, Anna Stichbury, Llew Summers, Cynthia Taylor, Peter Wallers, Mike Weston, Melissa Young.
Where to eat: Non Solo Pizza is located behind the gallery and there are numerous cafés and restaurants along Parnell Road.
What else to do nearby: Visit other galleries in Parnell or browse the boutiques; visit the Auckland War Memorial Museum; wander through the Parnell Rose Gardens.

Pierre Peeters Gallery (D)

Address: *Habitat Courtyard,*
251 Parnell Road, Parnell
Phone number: *(09) 377 4832*
Website: *www.ppg.net.nz*
Gallery Directors: *Pierre Peeters and*
Rachelle Pedersen
Opening times: *10.30 am to 5 pm Monday*
to Friday; 10.30 am to 4 pm Saturday;
12 pm to 4 pm Sunday.
Admission charges: *Free*
Guided tours: *On request*
Wheelchair access: *Yes*
Toilets: *Yes*

The Pierre Peeters Gallery is situated in the arts precinct of Parnell. It specialises in traditional, modern and contemporary New Zealand painters.

Their stable of artists is quite diverse, varying from the geometric abstract work of painter-composer Shannon Novak, whose individual pieces are teamed with music of his own composition, so a painting is heard as well as viewed, to the works of Gareth Price, who depicts surrealist juxtapositions of highly detailed objects and scenes, often mixing the mundane with the surprising. The gallery presents monthly exhibitions ranging from emerging to established artists. It also has regular shows from the established abstractionist Harry Wong, who is well known for his symbolic work from the 1960s, and the renowned Pacific realist Mark Cross.

Collection: Jean Horsley, Ralph Hotere
Exhibition schedule: Monthly
Artists represented: Alan Taylor, Andrew Hall, Anya Whitlock, Baye Riddell, Brent Hayward, Carl Foster, Gareth Price, Harry Wong, Mark Cross, Mike Morgan, Richard Boyd Dunlop, Sean Kerrigan, Shannon Novak.
Where to eat: Parnell Village offers a wide selection of cafés, bars and restaurants, all of a high quality.
What else to do nearby: Visit other galleries in Parnell; shop for antiques or fashion; explore the Auckland Domain, the Winter Gardens and the Auckland War Memorial Museum.

Pierre Peeters Gallery

Sanderson Contemporary Art (D)

Address: *251 Parnell Road, Parnell*
Phone number: *(09) 374 4476*
Website: *www.sanderson.co.nz*
Gallery Director: *Kylie Sanderson*
Opening times: *10.30 am to 5.30 pm Monday to Friday; 10.30 am to 5 pm Saturday; 11 am to 4 pm Sunday. On the second* *Thursday of each month Sanderson Contemporary Art and other Parnell galleries stay open until 7.30 pm for Late Night Art.*
Admission charges: *Free*
Guided tours: *No*
Wheelchair access: *Yes*
Toilets: *Yes, located in adjacent courtyard.*

Sanderson Contemporary Art is a progressive gallery focused on long-term representation of established New Zealand artists and fostering emerging talent. Specialising in contemporary New Zealand painting, sculpture and photography, Sanderson Contemporary Art presents new exhibitions every 2 to 3 weeks together with a dynamic programme of ancillary projects and events. With two rooms open to the public and over 20 represented artists, the gallery space offers a range of contemporary artworks for consideration. International shipping services are available on all purchases, as well as GST-exempt packages for overseas visitors.

Sanderson Contemporary Art

Collection: The gallery does not have a permanent collection.

Exhibition schedule: Refer to the gallery website for current and future exhibitions.

Artists represented: Andrew Barns-Graham, Josephine Cachemaille, Kevin Capon, Candi Dentice, Ted Dutch, Ben Foster, Liam Gerrard, Will Handley, Paul Hartigan, Ray Haydon, Linda Holloway, Cruz Jimenez, Gina Jones, Susanne Kerr, Clare Kim, Damien Kurth, Paul Martinson, Shintaro Nakahara, Yoshiko Nakahara, John Oxborough, P. J. Paterson, Alan Pearson, Martin Selman, Mark Ussher, Tracy Walker.

Where to eat: There are numerous cafés, restaurants and bars along Parnell Road.

What else to do nearby: Parnell is New Zealand's oldest suburb and Auckland's Creative Quarter. Famous for its galleries, cafés, restaurants and upmarket boutiques, Parnell's character village also features beautiful parks and remarkable historic buildings.

Seed Gallery (D)

Address: *Floor 1, 23A Crowhurst Street, Newmarket*
Phone number: *(09) 522 5360*
Website: *www.seedgallery.co.nz*
Gallery Directors: *Emma Pritchard and Kate Mullins*
Opening times: *10 am to 5 pm Tuesday to Friday; 10 am to 4 pm Saturday, or by appointment.*
Admission charges: *Free*
Guided tours: *No*
Wheelchair access: *No*
Toilets: *No*

Seed Gallery represents the best talent from a new generation of local artists and provides a positive and engaging experience for customers. The gallery displays a range of works by contemporary New Zealand artists working across the disciplines of painting, sculpture, ceramics, printmaking and photography.

Collection: A range of works by contemporary New Zealand artists.
Exhibition schedule: Monthly
Artists represented: Annie Smits Sandano, Louise McRae, Janna van Hasselt, Veronika Maser, John Appleton, Holly Shepheard, Stafford Allpress, John Pusateri, Sarah Williams, Aroha Lewin, Rebecca Thomson, Natasha Cantwell, Paddy O'Rourke, Mark Rayner, Richard Freestone, Tracey Black, Kim Lowe, Kristin Perrett.
Where to eat: Wise Cicada is just downstairs and Bambina (25 Teed Street) is across the road.
What else to do nearby: Newmarket is a shopping destination for fashion, homeware and specialty stores; watch a film at Rialto and Event movie cinemas; or walk up to the Auckland War Memorial Museum.

The Poi Room (D)

Address: *17 Osborne Street, Newmarket*
Phone number: *(09) 520 0399*
Website: *www.thepoiroom.co.nz*
Gallery Directors: *Melanie-Jane Smith and Clayton Smith*
Building: *Rialto Cinema and retail complex*
Opening times: *9.30 am to 5.30 pm Monday to Friday; 10 am to 5 pm Saturday; 11 am to 4 pm Sunday.*
Admission charges: *Free*
Guided tours: *No*
Wheelchair access: *Yes*
Toilets: *No*

The Poi Room holds a fabulous array of contemporary New Zealand art and design from emerging and established artists. There is a wide selection of paintings, prints, sculptural pieces, homeware, glassware, jewellery and ceramics – all made in New Zealand by New Zealand artists. Located in the heart of Newmarket, The Poi Room is set in a wonderfully accessible space and holds exhibitions, special events, wedding registers and online sales with post and packaging services available.

Collection: The gallery does not have a permanent collection.

Exhibition schedule: Approximately six exhibitions a year.

Artists represented: Shane Hansen, Lester Hall, Tracey Tawhiao, Te Rongo Kirkwood, Kate Barton, Katie Gold, Ross McCabe, Amanda Shanley, Penny Stotter, Brad Novak, Cynthia Taylor, Tony Ogle, Anna Church, Todd Douglas, Whiu Waata, Michele Bryant, Katie Brown, Tony Harrington, Ruth Baird, Justin Ferguson, Paula Coulthard, Genevieve Packer, Liam Barr, Tracey Williams, Peter Latham.

Where to eat: There are a number of cafés on Osborne and Teed Streets, including Altezano, The Teed Street Larder and Bambina.

What else to do nearby: Shopping on Osborne, Teed and Nuffield Streets; visit the Auckland War Memorial Museum and the Auckland Domain.

TSB Bank Wallace Arts Centre (P)

Address: The Pah Homestead, 72A Hillsborough Road, Hillsborough
Phone number: (09) 639 2010
Website: www.tsbbankwallaceartscentre.org.nz
Gallery Director: Sir James Wallace
Building: Historic Pah Homestead, built between 1877 and 1879.
Opening times: 10 am to 3 pm Tuesday to Friday; 10 am to 5 pm Saturday, Sunday and public holidays (excluding Mondays).
Admission charges: Free
Guided tours: 1.30 pm Tuesday to Friday, free of charge.
Wheelchair access: Yes
Toilets: Yes

The TSB Bank Wallace Arts Centre at the Pah Homestead is Auckland's new cultural destination. Located in the picturesque Monte Cecilia Park, the arts centre opened to the public in August 2010 and receives over 10,000 visitors every month. The Pah Homestead was fully restored by the Auckland Council together with support from TSB Bank and is the new home of the Wallace Arts Trust and its collection. The vision of the Trust is to simultaneously support, promote and expose New Zealand contemporary artists, while providing the wider public with an inimitable cultural and historical resource of contemporary New Zealand art free. The arts centre hosts a changing programme of free exhibitions curated from the collection, as well as regional touring exhibitions. It holds ongoing community education programmes targeting Auckland schools and the wider public. A partnership between the Trust and the University of Otago provides an artist-in-residence programme and allows for exhibitions to be curated from the Hocken Library. The Auckland Decorative and Fine Arts Society and its members provide ongoing support to the arts centre through the provision of volunteer docents.

Collection: The Wallace Arts Trust owns the strongest collection in any hands of a number of senior artists, such as Sir Toss Woollaston and Philip Trusttum, and also of many emerging and mid-career artists. It also has significant holdings of many other well-known artists. In addition, the Trust has initiated over 80 commissions ranging from Pat Hanly stained glass windows to Terry Stringer sculptures.

TSB Bank Wallace Arts Centre

Exhibition schedule: Major exhibitions are held in the Drawing Room and Ballroom of 2 months' duration, and minor exhibitions of approximately 1 to 2 months in smaller galleries, while the foyers and galleries are dedicated to audio visual displays and the continuous rotation of recent aquisitions.

Artists represented: Over 1000 artists are represented in the collection to date.

Where to eat: The in-house café, PAH, is operated by Dawsons, renowned Auckland caterers.

What else to do nearby: Take a guided map of Monte Cecilia Park and identify rare exotic trees.

The Pah Homestead was built between 1877 and 1879 for the Auckland businessman James Williamson. It was established as Williamson's 'gentleman's residence' and was one of the largest houses of the period. William Hart, an early Auckland settler, purchased the original 162-hectare property from local Maori in 1843. The grounds have significant cultural significance for local iwi as an area that once contained the Whataroa Pa. In 1870 the land was sold to Thomas Russell before James Williamson bought the property. The Bank of New Zealand gained ownership of the homestead in 1888, following Williamson's death, and leased it to the Anglican Church. It was later purchased by the Sisters of Mercy in 1913. In more recent times, the homestead became known as the Monte Cecilia House and was utilised to serve social needs, as an orphanage, a novitiate house, boarding school and for emergency housing.

Waiheke Community Art Gallery (P)

Address: *2 Korora Road, Oneroa, Waiheke Island*
Phone number: *(09) 372 9907*
Website: *www.waihekeartgallery.org.nz*
Gallery Director: *Linda Chalmers*
Building: *Artworks complex*

Opening times: *10 am to 4 pm daily.*
Admission charges: *Free*
Guided tours: *By appointment*
Wheelchair access: *Yes*
Toilets: *Yes*

The Waiheke Community Art Gallery is situated at the entrance to Oneroa in the Artworks complex. Walk into this gallery with its unassuming exterior and experience a range of diverse and inspiring art of national and international importance that you would never expect to find on a small island. Acclaimed artists from Waiheke and all around New Zealand exhibit here regularly. Every 4 weeks there is a new collection of eclectic, iconic and stimulating art on show, including national exhibitions of painting, ceramics, jewellery and sculpture alongside the creativity of Waiheke's own resident artists. The gallery's activities also extend to outdoor events, like the staggeringly beautiful biennial Headland: Sculpture on the Gulf exhibition on the Matiatia Walkway; an Artist in Residence programme; an annual summer school; book launches; youth exhibitions; environmental awareness and creating gala occasions with an arts focus. The gallery shop stocks high quality applied arts from Waiheke and throughout New Zealand.

Collection: Selected maquettes from previous Headland: Sculpture on the Gulf exhibitions.
Exhibition schedule: Changing programme every 4 weeks across three exhibition spaces.
Artists represented: Various. Refer to the gallery website for a list of artists.
Where to eat: Oneroa village offers a selection of cafés, bars and restaurants.
What else to do nearby: Check out Whittaker's Musical Museum; browse the Oneroa village shops.

Warwick Henderson Gallery (D)

Address: 32 Bath Street, Parnell
Phone number: (09) 309 7513
Website: www.warwickhenderson.co.nz
Gallery Director: Warwick Henderson, Anne Gifford (Manager)
Building: Single, purpose-built award-winning building.
Opening times: 10 am to 5.30 pm Tuesday to Friday; 10 am to 4 pm Saturday.
Admission charges: Free
Wheelchair access: First floor only
Toilets: No

In 1988 the Warwick Henderson Gallery moved from central Auckland to a new purpose-built gallery in Parnell. The gallery specialises in fine contemporary and period New Zealand art. It represents many prominent New Zealand artists, including Fatu Feu'u, Robyn Kahukiwa, Philippa Blair and Eion Stevens. The gallery has exhibited over 200 group and solo shows, including retrospectives of Trevor Moffitt, Dame Louise Henderson, Keith Patterson and Kase Jackson. It has also curated unique shows such as The Toy in Art and Naive Art, The Automobile in Art and Early New Zealand Photography. The gallery prides itself on integrity and service, and specialises in advice regarding the purchase, appraisal and valuation of investment and fine art. With over 30 years' experience, the gallery provides valuation services for insurance with all works sold by the gallery being guaranteed. Certificates of valuation and authenticity are issued with every piece. Shipping and insurance can be arranged both within New Zealand and internationally.

Collection: Don Binney, Colin McCahon, John Gibb, John Weeks, Pat Hanly, A. E. Aldis, Margaret Stoddart, Maud Sherwood and quality artworks from leading estates and collections.
Exhibition schedule: Monthly
Artists represented: Alexander Bartleet, Philippa Blair, Grant Corbishley, Rozi Demant, Fatu Feu'u, Viky Garden, Annette Isbey, Robyn Kahukiwa, Haneui Kim, Tyrone Layne, Amy Melchior,

Jenny Rendall, April Shin, Eion Stevens, Justin Summerton, Joanna Upperton, Nick Wall, Mark Wooller.

Where to eat: There are numerous cafés, restaurants and bars along Parnell Road.

What else to do nearby: Parnell's creative quarter includes many galleries and design stores; take a walk through the beautiful Parnell Rose Gardens.

Zealandia Sculpture Garden (S)

Address: 138 Mahurangi West Road (near Puhoi), RD3, Warkworth
Phone number: (09) 422 0099
Website: www.zealandiasculpturegarden.co.nz
Gallery Director: Tim McWhannell
Building: Private residence and gardens

Opening times: By appointment only
Admission charges: Refer to the Zealandia Sculpture Garden website for current fees.
Guided tours: By appointment
Wheelchair access: Yes
Toilets: Yes

Zealandia Sculpture Garden is the privately owned North Auckland garden and residence of renowned New Zealand sculptor Terry Stringer. The garden surprises the viewer with a vision in the pastoral New Zealand landscape. Created by the artist, the site comprises a gallery building made in the New Zealand shed idiom surrounded by farmland. The spaces form a theatre for the dramatic appearances of the sculpture.

Collection: Zealandia Sculpture Garden is a permanent collection.

Exhibition schedule: The sculpture garden features exhibitions from November to the end of March each year by prior appointment.

Artist represented: Terry Stringer

Where to eat: A selection of cafés and restaurants is available in Puhoi, Warkworth and Matakana, all located within a short drive.

What else to do nearby: Visit Puhoi Bohemian Village Museum, the Puhoi Valley Cheese Shop and Café; indulge in a tasting at Ascension Wine Estate; view the work at Morris & James Pottery; enjoy the natural beauty of Tawharanui Regional Park, Wenderholm Regional Park and the beaches at Orewa and Omaha.

Zealandia Sculpture Garden

Waikato

ArtsPost Galleries and Shop (P)

Address: *120 Victoria Street, Hamilton*
Phone number: *(07) 838 6928*
Website: *www.artspost.co.nz*
Gallery Coordinator: *Marion Manson*
Building: *Formerly the Post and Telegraph offices built in 1901, it is now a New Zealand*

Historic Places Trust Category II listed building.
Opening times: *10 am to 4.30 pm daily.*
Admission charges: *Free*
Guided tours: *No*
Wheelchair access: *Yes*
Toilets: *Yes*

ArtsPost is in one of Hamilton's most prominent heritage buildings in the heart of the city and is managed by the Waikato Museum. It aims to showcase the best in local art throughout their shop and galleries and is dedicated to developing and promoting artists, as well as growing a dynamic and supportive environment for the arts in the Waikato region. There is a wide variety of stock including works in glass, ceramic, textiles, painting, weaving, photography and jewellery. The gallery consists of a wide space encompassing three exhibition rooms and a large shop area.

Collection: ArtsPost does not have a permanent collection.
Exhibition schedule: Exhibitions are held over a 5-week period thus ensuring there is always something new on display.
Artists represented: Peter Collis, John Parker, de Flute Glass, Robin Lloyd, Sue Roots, Kate Hill, Heather Olesen, Colleen Ryan-Priest, Di Tocker, Marti Wong, Chris Jones, Ian Blackwell, Rob Kear, Julie Collis, Purses NZ, Kia Kaha Clothing, Jo Gallagher, Maureen Harte.
Where to eat: There are many options, including The River Kitchen, Palate, Furnace Bay & Nightclub, Keystone Monteiths Bar, Momento Espresso, Scotts Epicurean.
What else to do nearby: Visit Waikato Museum (next door); Skycity Casino; take a walk by the river nearby.

Baffin Street Gallery (D)

Address: *812 Baffin Street, Pirongia*
Phone number: *(07) 871 9890*
Website: *www.baffinstreetgallery.co.nz*
Gallery Director: *Hilary Ramage*
Opening times: *When the flag is displayed*

outside or by appointment.
Admission charges: *Free*
Guided tours: *On request*
Wheelchair access: *Yes*
Toilets: *If requested, in adjoining house.*

This gallery specialises in artists' prints. It is located on SH39, which is the southern approach road to Pirongia, a village nestled below Pirongia Mountain. Here you will find work from many New Zealand printmakers and a few local painters and photographers. They also carry work from a select few printmakers from Scotland and the United States of America. In addition there is a selection of handmade artists' books, sculptural pieces and glassware.

Collection: While the gallery does not have a permanent collection there are a number of works by Nan Mulder and Charles Cohan. This gallery is Nan Mulder's only outlet in New Zealand. Her processes are predominantly mezzotint and screen print.
Exhibition schedule: There is an ongoing exhibition of work by the artists represented. Throughout the year there are visiting artists who exhibit their work and take a weekend workshop. In 2011 those artists included: Terrie Reddish, botanical drawing; Anna Nelson, making an artist's travel journal; Professor Charles Cohan from the University of Hawai'i, multilayered printmaking without a press; and Harry Hart, acrylic painting.
Artists represented: Campbell Smith, Charles Cohan, Ruth Davey, Marty Vreede, Nan Mulder, Tom Davidson, Hilary Ramage, Carole Shepheard, Jane Siddall, Ron van der Vlugt, Terrie Reddish, Anna Nelson, Harry Hart, Kathy Watson, Kate Hill, Laura Hudson, Janice Meadows, Michelle Bocock, Jenny Scown, Julie Mello, Sue Kinloch, Miriam Saphira, Sue Roots, Prue MacDougall, Julienne Francis and others.
Where to eat: Pirongia village features Persimmon Tree Café and Little Clydesdale.
What else to do nearby: View Birdsong Gallery; visit Pirongia Historic Visitor Centre (museum with information about the land wars and the mountain fairies); go walking on Pirongia Mountain; drive around the mountain to the coastal towns of Raglan or Kawhia. Download a Pirongia Trails Brochure at www.pirongia.org.nz.

GibbsLang Contemporary Art Gallery and Studio (D)

Address: *555 Matangi Road, RD 4, Hamilton*
Phone number: *(07) 829 5909 or 027 248 4884*
Website: *www.gibbslang.co.nz (new website under construction)*
Gallery Director: *Catherine Lang*
Building: *Purpose-built, single-level contemporary art space*
Opening times: *10 am to 5 pm most days,*

weekends and public holidays, or by appointment. Phone first or visit when the open sign is displayed.
Admission charges: *Free*
Guided tours: *On request, groups welcome.*
Wheelchair access: *Yes*
Toilets: *Yes, also wheelchair accessible.*

The GibbsLang Contemporary Art Gallery and Studio is situated among about 3 hectares of gardens, sculptures, trees and farmland just outside Matangi village, 10 minutes from both Hamilton city and airport, and 15 minutes from Cambridge. The gallery is part of a purpose-built domestic dwelling and art complex designed by reputable architect Noel Jessop. The gallery provides art tuition and also has an art leasing service.

Collection: The gallery's collection features work by Colin Gibbs – contemporary prints, photographs and paintings on canvas and paper, in oils, acrylics and inks, ranging in size from small works to large multiple canvases.
Exhibition schedule: Exhibitions change every 2 months.
Artists represented: Donn Ratana (painting, drawing and sculpture), Jenny Taris (pottery), Jenny Chapman (photography), Marjorie Gibbs (photography).
Where to eat: Try Woodside Estate Café (3-minutes' drive), The Woodbox Winery Restaurant & Bar (10-minutes' drive), Red Cherry Café and Coffee Roasters (10-minutes' drive).
What else to do nearby: This gallery is part of 'The Scene Between' – eight unique Waikato sites between the river and the hills and includes The Sculpture Park @ Waitakaruru Arboretum, Inspirit Studio & Gallery and Tamahere Country Market (third Saturday of the month). Download 'The Scene Between' map from http://hamilton.co.nz/file/fileid/17999.

Artist Colin Gibbs was born in Whanganui. He spent his childhood in the shadows of the Parapara hills and alongside the Whanganui River. Colin specialised in art at Palmerston North Teachers College from 1968 to 1969 under the tuition of Frank Davis and Ray Thorburn. During earlier years Colin completed paintings that presented social and political messages related to issues such as Māori land claims and New Zealand's involvement in the Vietnam War. More recent work explores biculturalism, relationships with our land, and social commentary. From late 1970 to 1998 Colin completed only one painting. He destroyed almost all his early works – only one of these survives and is in the collection of the Sarjeant Gallery, Whanganui. Paintings are known for their intensity of colour. His series on James K Baxter's poem 'Song of the Years' is well known.

Heritage Gallery (D)

Address: *85A Victoria Street, SH1, Cambridge*
Phone number: *(07) 827 4346*
Website: *www.heritagegallery.co.nz*
Gallery Director: *Sandra Webb*
Opening times: *9.30 am to 5 pm Monday to Friday; 9.30 am to 4 pm Saturday,*
Sunday and public holidays.
Admission charges: *Free*
Guided tours: *By appointment*
Wheelchair access: *Yes*
Toilets: *Public toilets nearby, within 20 metres.*

Established in 1995 Heritage Gallery showcases the excellent quality and the depth of creative arts in New Zealand. Ideally situated on SH1 in the picturesque town of Cambridge,

Heritage Gallery has become a favourite stop for international and Kiwi travellers. Owner Sandra Webb has a background as a potter. Her understanding of the mechanics of craft and the unique demands on being creative has been instrumental in developing relationships in the art world. The eclectic range on display includes original art, quality prints, studio glass, ceramics, handmade jewellery and designer garments. The selection is unique and ever evolving.

Collection: The gallery does not have a permanent collection.
Exhibition schedule: Monthly exhibitions of featured art.
Artists represented: Painters: Brian Strong, Jane Galloway, J. K. Reed, Rodney Hamel, Carole Hughes, Tony Lewis, Megan Daniels, John Ruth. Jewellers: Gavan Riley, Mieke van Dam. Potters: John Crawford, Fiona Tunnicliffe, Tony Sly, Peter Shearer, Kim Morgan, Craig Fletcher. Glass Artists: Garry Nash, Peter Viesnik, Katie Brown, David Traub, Lynden Over, Shona Firman, Keith Mahy.
Where to eat: For great coffee try In Stone Café next door, and there are numerous good restaurants and cafés in town.
What else to do nearby: Cambridge is an easy town to walk around and there are signposted historic and scenic walks as well as boutique shopping. Excellent antique shops, equine stud tours, the famous Maungatautari Ecological Island reserve, Lake Karapiro and a good golf course make it an ideal weekend destination.

Inspirit Studio & Gallery (D)

Address: 360 Pencarrow Road, Tamahere, Hamilton
Phone number: (07) 856 3170 or 027 438 6416
Website: www.inspirit.co.nz
Gallery Director: Jenny Scown
Opening times: 10 am to 4 pm Saturday and Sunday. Tuesday to Friday when the open sign is displayed outside, or by appointment.
Admission charges: Free
Guided tours: Yes, for groups of 10 or more.
Wheelchair access: Yes
Toilets: Yes

Inspirit Studio & Gallery is a spacious contemporary gallery and stunning sculpture lawn located halfway between Hamilton and Cambridge in a beautiful rural setting. On display is a diverse range of original art and design representing not only emerging and established artists from throughout the country, but also many leading local artists. The gallery features photography, painting, printmaking, glass, jewellery, furniture, ceramics, fashion, indoor and outdoor sculpture and mixed media works, as well as pre-loved vintage pieces.

Inspirit has changing exhibitions and the multifunctional space is also used for other creative events and workshops. It also offers guided art tours for groups and Inspirit is part of 'The Scene Between', a popular art and culture trail featuring the best of art, food, wine, coffee, sculpture parks and gardens in the region. Download 'The Scene Between' map from http://hamilton.co.nz/file/fileid/17999.

Inspirit Studio & Gallery

Collection: The gallery does not have a permanent collection.
Exhibition schedule: Regular changing exhibitions during the year. Refer to the gallery website for current and future exhibitions.
Artists represented: Joan Fear, Santie Cronje-English, Rachel Olsen, Rebecca Meyer, Renata Przynoga-Cousins, Jane Galloway, Ian Webster, Colleen Ryan-Priest, Di Tocker, Jenny Scown, Jane Siddall, Aroha Wikotu, Christine Rabarts, Ciane Lawrey, Chris Meek, Marti Wong, Robin Cuff, Kate Hill, Joan Travaglia, Peter Radley, Jocelyn Pratt, Nick Dryden, Bruce Young, Tanya Finlayson, Dianne Dudfield.
Where to eat: The gallery is surrounded by award-winning cafés and restaurants: Woodside Estate Café, The Woodbox Winery Restaurant & Bar, Red Cherry Café and Coffee Roasters and Punnet are all only a few minutes' drive away.
What else to do nearby: Visit The Sculpture Park @ Waitakaruru Arboretum; wine tasting at Mystery Creek Wines; enjoy Hamilton Gardens and Moondance Manor Gardens; play at Lochiel Golf Club or Narrows Golf Club; mark the date for the Tamahere Country Market (third Saturday of the month).

Kura Gallery (D)

Address: 47A Heuheu Street, Taupo
Phone number: (07) 377 4068
Website: www.kura.co.nz
Gallery Director: Carol Hunter
Opening times: 10 am to 4 pm daily.

Admission charges: Free
Guided tours: No
Wheelchair access: No
Toilets: No

Contemporary New Zealand art created by New Zealand artists is the focus at Kura ('treasure' in Maori) and you will be surprised by the wealth of treasures to be found in this small, unique gallery. Just 5 minutes' walk from the shores of beautiful Lake Taupo, sitting among other galleries and cafés in the central city, this gem of a gallery represents more than 70 artists from throughout the country and includes some of New Zealand's best-loved artists and emerging talent. The works feature an eclectic mix of media, including shell (such as paua), pounamu (greenstone or jade) and native wood, which proudly speak of who we are as a culture. The works range from carving, weaving, ceramics, sculpture and jewellery to original paintings and prints.

Collection: The gallery does not have a permanent collection.
Exhibition schedule: The gallery does not hold exhibitions.
Artists represented: Brian Adam, James Atutahi, Ruth Baird, Liam Barr, Nick Bradford, Russell Brown, Simon Morrison-Deaker, Fane Flaws, Darryl Frost, Fiona Gedson, Hannah Jensen, Robyn Kahukiwa, Te Kaha, Jess Paraone, Kerry Thompson, Zoya Beri.
Where to eat: Replete Café is next door to the gallery.
What else to do nearby: Visit the rose gardens; take the heritage walk from museum to boat harbour; go trout fishing; and many other activities in the area.
Refer to Taupo i-SITE www.greatlaketaupo.com/new-zealand/i_sites for information.

Moko Artspace (D)

Address: *24 Pye Place, Hot Water Beach, Whitianga, Coromandel Peninsula*
Phone number: *(07) 866 3367*
Website: *www.moko.co.nz*
Gallery Directors: *Simon Buchanan and Sonya Corlett*
Building: *Purpose-built gallery, shop and sculpture garden*

Opening times: *9 am to 5 pm daily. Hours may vary throughout the season.*
Admission charges: *Free*
Guided tours: *Staff are available to answer any questions about exhibited work or artists.*
Wheelchair access: *Yes*
Toilets: *Public toilets at the beach opposite the gallery.*

Moko Artspace

Moko is an artspace at Hot Water Beach which houses an impressive contingent of New Zealand-made products from serious craft art to a lighter selection of kiwiana, including contemporary gifts, jewellery, art, glass, sculpture and homeware. The gallery displays the work of many local artists, as well as a rotating selection of national artists. The collection includes stunning glass sculpture, an extensive range of jewellery, ceramics, wood, paintings and prints, weaving and textiles.

Collection: The gallery does not have a permanent collection, although some sculptures are part of the landscaped garden.
Exhibition schedule: Continuous
Artists represented: David Traub, Evelyn Dunstan, Garth Dobney, Ron van der Vlugt, Jason Svendsen, Justin Culina, Amber Smith, Robyn Lewis, Leonie Sharp, Greg Straight, Alan Wehipeihana, James Atutahi, Dean Raybould, Hope Gibbons, Daniel Kirsch, Russell Brown, Bruce Young, Mary Paton, Bruno Gaebler, Ché Vincent, Martin J akowitsch, Sophie Lewis-Smith, Maike Barteldres, Hannah Clayton, Liz Kendrik.
Where to eat: Hot Waves Café is next door or Colenso Country Café & Shop on SH25.
What else to do nearby: Hot Water Beach is officially one of the top 10 beaches in the world and is a popular place to visit at any time of the year, but especially at Christmas when pohutukawa are in full bloom. Try surfing, fishing, diving and the famous hot pools in the sand. For a couple of hours either side of low tide simply dig your toes in the sand until you find a hot spot where the naturally heated mineral water is flowing. Dig yourself a pool and relax. When the tide is high, try kayaking; visit Cathedral Cove; take guided bush walks or go horse trekking.

Sinclair Barclay Gallery (A)

Address: 59 Duke Street, Cambridge
Phone number: (07) 827 8415
Website: The gallery does not have a website.
Gallery Directors: Wayne Sinclair and Robyn Barclay
Opening times: 10 am to 4.30 pm Monday to Friday; 10 am to 2 pm Saturday.
Admission charges: Free
Guided tours: No
Wheelchair access: Yes
Toilets: No

This gallery displays works in oils and acrylics by artists Wayne Sinclair and Robyn Barclay. At any one time there are up to 60 paintings on display. Their pieces range from traditional and impressionist scenes of New Zealand to many overseas studies from the artists' travels. Sinclair Barclay will send paintings around New Zealand for you to view in your home before you decide to purchase.

Collection: The gallery does not have a permanent collection.
Exhibition schedule: The gallery does not have an exhibition schedule.
Artists represented: Wayne Sinclair, Robyn Barclay
Where to eat: There are numerous cafés and restaurants nearby.

What else to do nearby: Shop at Cambridge Farmers' Market (Saturday); walk the heritage and boutique trails and the Cambridge Tree Trail; visit Maungatautari Ecological Island reserve to see native wildlife (including kiwis). Refer to Cambridge i-SITE at www.cambridge.co.nz/site-map for more information.

Studio 73 (A)

Address: 73 Wordsworth Street, Leamington, Cambridge
Phone number: (07) 823 9474
Website: www.heatheranneatkins.com
Gallery Director: Heather Anne Atkins
Building: Private residence and gallery
Opening times: 10 am to 4 pm Tuesday to Friday; Saturday and Sunday by appointment.

Admission charges: Free
Guided tours: By appointment, please phone first.
Wheelchair access: On request, if arranged prior to visiting.
Toilets: Not for general public use but available for tours.

Studio 73 is the home-based working gallery of ceramic artist and painter Heather Anne Atkins, who has a unique art history going back to the early 1980s. Through the glazed doors of the gallery entrance a wide variety of work is on show. The artist is often working on pieces in clear view of visitors and enjoys the resulting interaction with them. On the ceramic side of her work, the artist takes pleasure in working with porcelain and sculptural clays and tends to focus on pieces inspired by New Zealand. Birds, wildlife, farm and domestic animals are prominent in her work; however, delicate porcelain bowls, teapots and figurative work also have their place. Canvas acrylic paintings, both representational and contemporary, continue her New Zealand theme. Her most recent 'Wine Series' encompassing grapes, vintages, tasting notes and related background scenes has a loyal following in other galleries. Heather Anne hopes to continue her artwork for many more years and relishes every moment given to creating a new piece.

Collection: Pottery piece presented to Princess Diana, at Government House during the 1983 Royal New Zealand Tour. The artist was commissioned to create three ceramic artworks for the managerial offices of the Bank of New Zealand Tower (Queen Street, Auckland) in 1987. She was also commissioned to paint a large 9-metre fresco for the Ascension Wine Estate (Matakana), *The Meeting of Bacchus and Ariadne*, as featured on nationwide TV3 News (30 March 2002).
Exhibition schedule: Regular exhibitions throughout the country.
Artist represented: Heather Anne Atkins
Where to eat: Cambridge has many good cafés. Try Onyx Café and Bar, GPO Bar & Brasserie and Café Irresistiblue (Monavale Blueberries).
What else to do nearby: Cambridge is an easy town to walk around and there are signposted historic and scenic walks as well as boutique shopping. Excellent antique shops, equine stud tours, the famous Maungatautari Ecological Island reserve, Lake Karapiro and a good golf course make it an ideal weekend destination.

Taupo Museum

Taupo Museum (P)

Address: Story Place, Taupo
Phone number: (07) 376 0414
Website: www.taupomuseum.co.nz
Gallery Director: Luisa Haines
Opening times: 10 am to 4.30 pm daily.
Admission charges: Free to children,

Taupo residents and ratepayers;
visiting adults $5, seniors/students $3.
Guided tours: 2 pm Sunday
Wheelchair access: Yes
Toilets: Yes

Taupo Museum, via a balanced programme of changing exhibitions, aims to provide opportunities for visitors to view, study and enjoy a diversity of art, craft, design and other exhibits encompassing a wide range of media, styles and subject matter. The museum has a programme of changing exhibitions, which aims to broaden and build its appeal, encourage repeat visits and develop new audiences, including cross-generational and cross-cultural groups, families and those with special needs. It is representative and mindful of the community in which it operates and continues to develop its reputation both locally and nationally as a centre for the arts.

Collection: The museum has a small collection of work from local artists.
Exhibition schedule: Refer to the gallery website for current and future exhibitions.
Where to eat: There are many good cafés nearby.
What else to do nearby: Visit the rose gardens; take the heritage walk from museum to boat harbour; go trout fishing; and many other activities in the area. Refer to Taupo i-SITE www.greatlaketaupo.com/new-zealand/i_sites for information.

Thames Society of Arts (P)

Address: *Old North School, 604 Tararu Road, Thames*
Phone number: *(07) 868 9192*
Website: *www.thamesinfo.co.nz/activities*
Gallery Director: *There is no permanent director.*
Building: *Formerly the Thames Old North School.*
Opening times: *10 am to 4 pm daily.*
Admission charges: *Free*
Guided tours: *No*
Wheelchair access: *Yes*
Toilets: *Yes*

This is an incorporated society formed by a group of local artists in 1973. The aim was to have a place where artists could create, display and sell their works. These include oil paintings, acrylics and watercolours. There is a large selection of unframed watercolours, which are easy for a traveller to transport. Many of the members create artworks in other mediums, such as woodwork, fibre, pottery, and jewellery and greetings cards, offering a wide variety with appeal to both local and overseas tourists. The Old North School is the home of the society and is located 3 minutes north of the Thames town centre on the main road that follows the coast towards Coromandel township.

Collection: The society does not have a permanent collection.
Exhibition schedule: Occasional exhibitions are held by the society.
Artists represented: Dennis Raines, Trish Hamilton, Marianne Braithwaite, Maureen Cann, Ian Webster (pottery), Donna Hansby (fibre), Pamela Plummer (painting and pottery), Mike Finn, Jan McIvor, Joanne Mahoney (art cards), Peter Coatsworth (woodcarving), Peter Ripley (woodturning), Barbara von Sieda, Sarah Peck (wire sculpture), Eunice Braithwaite, Helen Stuart (copper work), Helena du Preez (pottery).
Where to eat: There is a variety of cafés and eateries in Thames town centre.
What else to do nearby: Visit the historic mine sites; go boating and fishing; take scenic drives up the valley and enjoy a bush walk.

The Sculpture Park @ Waitakaruru Arboretum (S)

Address: *207 Scotsman Valley Road, Tauwhare, Hamilton*
Phone number: *(07) 824 0733*
Website: *www.sculpturepark.co.nz*
Gallery Directors: *Dorothy and John Wakeling*
Building: *The sculpture park is located within the grounds of the Waitakaruru Arboretum.*
Opening times: *10 am to 6.30 pm daily*
(summer); 10 am to 5 pm daily (winter).
Admission charges: *Adults (15+) $10, children (5–14 years) $5.*
Guided tours: *On request*
Wheelchair access: *There are hard base roads throughout most of the park, making for easy accessibility.*
Toilets: *Yes*

The Sculpture Park @ Waitakaruru Arboretum is a unique destination in the Waikato region that offers visitors 2 kilometres of walkway through lush vegetation in a rehabilitated ex-quarry. The park is open all year round and features three annual exhibitions. All exhibitions are archived and can be viewed on the events and exhibitions tab on the website. New Zealand artists, from emerging to senior practitioners, are on display with over 60 works exhibited throughout the 17-hectare park. All works are for sale and all commissions go to the Waikato Sculpture Trust, a registered charitable trust.

The exhibitions are managed by the Waikato Sculpture Trust whose aim is to create the 'Art Place to Be'. The trust believes that sculpture matters and wishes to encourage its development as a widely appreciated genre in New Zealand. This is supported by a diverse and growing group of artists from throughout the country. The trust employs a guest curator to plan each new exhibition; innovation and experimentation are welcome with particular emphasis on environmentally based artworks. The trust runs the Environmental Art Photography Challenge as part of this initiative (see the website for details).

Collection: C. K. Reynolds, *Absolute Divide*; Neville Parker, *Velvet Stampede*; Fatu Fe'u, *Tuitagaloa and Rongo*; Ian Boyle, *Aspiring*; Christian Nicolson, *Biggie (Spitfire)*; Bernie Harfleet, *Inglorious*; Niko Thomsen, *Cross*; John Ioane, *Pearliculture*.

Exhibition schedule: The park holds three exhibitions a year. Refer to the gallery website for current and future exhibitions.

Artists represented: Gareth Williams, Gregor Kregar, Lee Harrop, John Ioane, Kirsty Gardiner, Colleen Ryan-Priest, Murray Swan, John Edgar, Peter Lange, Aaron McConchie, Lucy Bucknall, Gaye Jurisich, Duncan Sargent, Jin Ling, Linda Pringle, Ian Boyle, Niko Thomsen, Christian Nicolson, Jocelyn Pratt, Karin Barr, Linda Bruce, Chris Mules, Ralph Price, Grant Palliser.

Where to eat: On-site Leaping Frog Café is open at weekends throughout the summer.

What else to do nearby: Refer to www.arterial.co.nz for local art venues.

Thornton Gallery (D)

Address: *298 Barton Street, Hamilton*
Phone number: *(07) 839 1325*
Website: *www.thorntongallery.co.nz*
Gallery Director: *Alex McPherson*
Opening times: *9.30 am to 5.30 pm Monday* *to Friday; 10 am to 4 pm Saturday and Sunday.*
Admission charges: *Free*
Guided tours: *By appointment*
Wheelchair access: *Yes*
Toilets: *On exhibition nights only*

Thornton Art Gallery is well known throughout the Waikato and Auckland regions and has been established for over 50 years. A wide range of styles and genres are on display and with over 100 artists exhibiting there are many unique and beautiful one-off pieces. The artworks are constantly changing as new pieces arrive every week. Along with original paintings by mainly New Zealand artists, Thornton Gallery sells prints and limited edition prints (both framed and unframed), ceramics, glass, wood, stone, bone and jewellery. Quality and integrity are important criteria for the works exhibited in this gallery. Thornton Gallery also has an extensive framing business on-site and are experienced in working with prints, photographs, originals, medals, T-shirts, needlework and tapa cloths to full museum grade conservation jobs.

Collection: The gallery does not have a permanent collection.
Exhibition schedule: Refer to the gallery website for current and future exhibitions.
Artists represented: Michael Smither, Peter Collis, Royce McGlashen, Jane Puckey,
Gaye Jurisich, Terry Prince, Fane Flaws, Blue-Tui, Lisa Ormsby, Collette Renee Fergus,
Sue Christie, Maureen Allison, Beverly Cameron, Vicki Axtens, Lauryne Hart, Bruce McLachlan,
Gary Tricker, Grant Simpson, Isaac Peterson, Nick Fedaeff, Brian Baxter, Lindsey Baker,
Brad Novak, Miranda Jane Caird, Ian Hamlin and Dick Frizzell.
Where to eat: There are many cafés nearby.
What else to do nearby: Lots of opportunities for shopping, wining and dining;
visit Skycity Casino; check out the Casabella Lane boutiques; take a relaxing
riverside walk.

Wallace Gallery Morrinsville (P)

Address: 167 Thames Street, Morrinsville
Phone number: (07) 889 7791
Website: www.morrinsvillegallery.org.nz
Gallery Director: Charlotte Giblin
Building: Formerly the old Morrinsville
Post Office
Opening times: 10 am to 4 pm Tuesday
to Sunday.
Admission charges: Free, donations
welcome.
Guided tours: Helpful volunteer staff can
assist visitors, if required.
Wheelchair access: Yes
Toilets: Yes, one with wheelchair access.

Established in October 2010, this stunning venue in the heart of the Waikato has new
exhibitions every 2 weeks in the Community Gallery and every month in the Main Gallery.
Three large exhibition spaces allow inspirational New Zealand art to be shown, including an
extensive selection of work from the Wallace Arts Trust Collection. The display of work from
the Wallace Arts Trust Collection changes every 2 months, ensuring a continual display of
interesting and creative pieces. Most artistic mediums are covered over a period of months
and the setting allows for workshops and lectures to be held within the inspiring interior.
Musical recitals, theatrical productions and other creative events take place periodically and
the regular exhibition previews are popular. The gallery also has a shop filled with local high
quality art and crafts. Latest news, events, images from the exhibitions and other information
can be found on the gallery website.

Collection: The Wallace Arts Trust Collection
Exhibition schedule: The Community Gallery has new works exhibited every 2 weeks. The
Main Gallery exhibits new works every 4 weeks and new pieces in the Wallace Arts Trust
Collection are exhibited every 8 to 10 weeks.
Artists represented: New Zealand artists
Where to eat: There are cafés in town.
What else to do nearby: Visit Morrinsville Heritage Centre; browse the numerous shops and
boutiques; drive 20 minutes to visit the Spa in Te Aroha, Firth Tower and Hobbiton Movie Set
and Farm Tours in Matamata.

Wallace Gallery Morrinsville

ZeaYou Gallery (D)

Address: *Cnr Heuheu and Ruapehu Streets, Taupo*
Phone number: *(07) 378 1361*
Website: *www.zeayou.com*
Gallery Director: *Dianne Campbell*
Opening times: *10 am to 5 pm Monday to* *Friday; 10 am to 3 pm Saturday; 11 am to 2 pm Sunday.*
Admission charges: *Free*
Guided tours: *No*
Wheelchair access: *Yes*
Toilets: *Yes*

ZeaYou Gallery is a vibrant space specialising in a diverse range of mediums including contemporary New Zealand art, showcasing paintings, limited edition prints, cast and blown glass, sculpture and jewellery. ZeaYou Gallery offers an enlightening insight into New Zealand's art scene.

Collection: The gallery does not have a permanent collection.
Exhibition schedule: Refer to the gallery website for current and future exhibitions.
Artists represented: Trevor J. Askin, Sean Crawford, Gail Edmonds, Matt Guild, Michelle Farrell, Shane Hansen, Bill Hayes, Jason Hicks, Yi Ming Lin, Glen Mills, Brad Novak, Sandy Rogers, Carole Shepheard, Carmen Simmonds, Richard Smith, Llew Summers, Cynthia Taylor, David Traub, Peter Wallers, Alan Waters, Yvonne Westra, Belinda Wilson.
Where to eat: The Brantry Restaurant (45 Rifle Range Road) is recommended.
What else to do nearby: Visit Kura Gallery; the rose gardens; Taupo Museum and the library; go trout fishing or take the heritage walk from the museum to the boat harbour. Refer to Taupo i-SITE www.greatlaketaupo.com/new-zealand/i_sites for information.

Bay of Plenty

4 Art Sake Gallery (D)

Address: 23 Pohutukawa Avenue,
Ohope Beach, Whakatane
Phone number: (07) 312 4223
Website: www.4artsake.co.nz
Gallery Director: Linda Fergusson
Building: The original Ohope Beach
Post Office
Opening times: 10 am to 6 pm Monday to
Thursday; 10 am to 7 pm Friday to Sunday
(summer). 10 am to 4 pm Monday to
Thursday; 10 am to 6 pm Friday to Sunday,
closed Tuesday (winter).
Admission charges: Free
Guided tours: No
Wheelchair access: Yes
Toilets: Yes

Every week visitors from all over the world applaud 4 Arts Sake Gallery as being one of the most beautiful galleries they have ever visited. Just 140 square metres inside with an 80-square-metre garden, it is overflowing with an abundance of treasures 90% of which are created by New Zealand artists. Fine art is predominant, but you will find lots of hidden gems ranging from three-dimensional sculpture and pristine glassware to jewellery and pop art. The gallery also displays genuine Maori whalebone carving, New Zealand paua (abalone shell) and New Zealand pounamu (greenstone or jade). Visiting 4 Arts Sake in seaside Ohope is a visual experience that lingers.

Collection: Jamie Boynton, *Te Oho* (The Awakening, 2009). This self-portrait received the Highly Commended Award at the 2009 Molly Morpeth Canaday Art Awards for painting and drawing.
Exhibition schedule: The gallery does not hold regular exhibitions.
Artists represented: Maree White, Fiona Gedson, Tallulah Belle Lautrec-Nunes, Wayne Vickers, Ross Lee, Jenny Cook-Battersby, Joanne Lenne, Keith Lewis, Pru Rangi, Susan Bunch, Tobi Dante, Gail Challenger, Peter Cramond, Bruce Young, Todd Harris, Lane Hawkins, Ron Reid, Blair Little.
Where to eat: Try Toi Toi Bar & Brasserie, Quay Café and Restaurant and Beach Haven Café.
What else to do nearby: The area offers plenty to do, or total relaxation, in a pristine beach environment with the most sunshine hours in New Zealand. There is a variety of water sports available, including waterskiing, sailing, kayaking, surfing, windsurfing and big-game fishing. Also try: White Island tours; bush walks; picnics in Mahy Reserve; or play a round of golf at the Ohope Golf Course.

4 Art Sake Gallery

Harrisons Gallery (D)

Address: *106 Eleventh Avenue, Tauranga*
Phone number: *(07) 578 9322*
Website: *www.harrisonsgallery.com*
Managing Director: *Gaye Carrothers*
Opening times: *9 am to 5 pm Monday to Friday; 10 am to 2 pm Saturday, or by appointment.*

Admission charges: *Free*
Guided tours: *Private viewings are available on request.*
Wheelchair access: *Yes, ramp to main entrance.*
Toilets: *Public toilets nearby, within 20 metres.*

Established in 1961, Harrisons Gallery is the Bay of Plenty's leading fine art gallery and one of Tauranga's oldest businesses. They offer a full range of art services: a fine art gallery; custom framing; art valuations and restorations; ArtBuzz Art School; art books and cards; and Tauranga's largest range of quality artist supplies. Their team of art consultants and technicians offer unrivalled expertise. The gallery represents over 30 local, national and international artists and runs a popular exhibition schedule. ArtBuzz Art School offers art classes for adults and kids of all ages, styles and abilities. Tutors include an array of local, national and international established artists. Harrisons' Master Framer is a qualified Guild Commended Framer and is a member of the New Zealand Institute of Picture Framers. Specialising in custom framing, including conservation and museum grade, this gallery has gained a reputation for framing difficult or unusual items. Harrisons specialise in the restoration of artworks and textiles, and offers independent valuations for insurance purposes or resale. They also offer free, no obligation, in-home consultations designed to take the guesswork out of art buying.

Collection: The gallery does not have a permanent collection.
Exhibition schedule: Refer to the gallery website for current and future exhibitions.
Artists represented: Murray Ayson, Talitha Brauchli, Nick Clegg, Lisa Christiansen, Dean Corbett, Paul Deacon, Mandy Hague, Shane Hansen, Mara Hermann, Ben Ho, Luke Hollis, Beverley Hollister-Jones, James Lawrence, Doreen McNeil, Mary Mulholland, Elliot Mason, Brad Novak, Michael Ponder, Richard Ponder, Richard Smith, Colin Unkovich, Peter Wallers, Antony Warnes, Nigel Wilson, Tim Wilson, Russell Winterburn, John Yardley.
Where to eat: There are several cafés nearby within 5 minutes' walk.
What else to do nearby: The central city and waterfront are only minutes away.

Tauranga Art Gallery Toi Tauranga (P)

Address: 108 Willow Street, Tauranga
Phone number: (07) 578 7933
Website: www.artgallery.org.nz
Gallery Director: Penelope Jackson
Building: In 1999 the former Bank of New Zealand building was purchased by the Tauranga Art Gallery Trust and converted to meet modern art gallery standards. The gallery opened to the public on 20 October 2007.

Opening times: 10 am to 4.30 pm daily; 1 pm to 4.30 pm Anzac Day. Closed Christmas Day, Boxing Day and New Year's Day.
Admission charges: Free, except for special events or exhibitions.
Guided tours: On request
Wheelchair access: Yes, there is a lift.
Toilets: Yes

The Tauranga Art Gallery Toi Tauranga is located in central Tauranga in the converted former Bank of New Zealand building. They hold up to six exhibitions at any one time, ranging from traditional to contemporary. Thousands of children visit the gallery for education and school holiday programmes every year, and for events ranging from floor talks to musical performances and book signings. The gallery is also a striking and interesting space as a function venue.

Collection: Edward Bullmore, Nigel Brown, Robin White.
Exhibition schedule: Schedule changes every 6 weeks. Refer to the gallery website for current and future exhibitions.
Artists represented: The gallery does not represent individual artists.
Where to eat: There are a number of local cafés in the area.
What else to do nearby: Visit historic The Elms House Museum and the Brain Watkins House Museum; stroll around the waterfront.

Tauranga Art Gallery Toi Tauranga

The Art Boutique (D)

Address: *514 Cambridge Road, Tauranga*
Phone number: *(07) 543 4932*
Website: *www.theartboutique.co.nz*
Gallery Directors: *John and Sylvia Harmsen*
Building: *The building is approximately 15 years old with beautiful macrocarpa-lined vaulted ceilings. It incorporates the doors and entranceway of the Holy Trinity Church of Tauranga built in 1875, which were saved when the original church was destroyed by fire some 25 years ago.*
Opening times: *9.30 am to 4 pm daily.*
Admission charges: *Free*
Guided tours: *No*
Wheelchair access: *Yes*
Toilets: *Yes, also has wheelchair access.*

This gallery focuses largely on artwork by local Bay of Plenty artists including painting, sculpture, ceramics, pottery and jewellery. There is also work by other New Zealand artists from outside of the area.

Collection: The gallery does not have a permanent collection.
Exhibition schedule: The gallery does not have an exhibition schedule.
Artists represented: Rob McGregor, Rosie Harper, Adrian Corry, Jenny Coker, Richard MacDonald, Margaret Fairs, Lis Eynon, Nick Eggleston, Mandy Williams, Sue Dent, Ben Barrett, Lynne Mathieson, Catherine Outwin, Bill Pritchard, Sylvia Kula, Peter Crammond, Viv Edwards, Linda Elliott, Emily Hill, Kate Jones Madill, Michelle Kirk, Rebecca Meyer, Mischelle O'Donnell, Suzanne Smith, Val Tubman, Alec Roy, Murray Garner, Dorothy Armstrong, Carolyn Turner, Lynda Powell, Jocelyn Burrell, Luanne Lawton.
Where to eat: There is a café on the premises.
What else to do nearby: There is a furniture maker and also a wood carver on the property. Both artisans have showrooms displaying their products.

The Art Boutique

ZOHAR Art & Design Gallery

ZOHAR Art & Design Gallery (D)

Address: 104 Maunganui Road,
Mount Maunganui
Phone number: (07) 574 7428
Website: www.zohar.co.nz
Gallery Directors: Sylvia and John Harmsen
Building: Situated in the Mount's Main Street shopping precinct with a dedicated area for the display of original artworks.

Opening times: 10 am to 5 pm Monday to Friday; 10 am to 4 pm Saturday and Sunday (early closing on Sunday throughout winter months).
Admission charges: Free
Guided tours: On request
Wheelchair access: Yes
Toilets: No

ZOHAR has been a landmark store in Mount Maunganui since 2003 and is often described as contemporary, stylish and with exclusive originals. ZOHAR features some of the most creative pieces made by New Zealand's best designers and artisans, as well as work from artists around the world. ZOHAR's mission is to promote the creativity and uniqueness of New Zealand people and their talents; over 90% of the artwork on display is New Zealand made. The gallery enjoys being able to display the works of our artisans and designers and encourages people to celebrate this uniqueness by taking pieces home with them.

Collection: Brett Taylor's bronze hammerhead shark and *Contemplative Man* in stonework; John Wolter's metal native birds and fauna; Grant Simpson's oil paintings of the Coromandel; Kerensa Clark's silver and gold collection of 'Love' jewellery; pounamu (greenstone or jade) jewellery by carvers Ross McCabe, Cherry Peeti-Tapurau, Greg Maitland, Ernesto Ovalle and David Oakes; Art By Huia, a collection of Maori-inspired feather ketes, mats and masks; Hayley Hamilton's collection of word art; limited edition photographs by Colin McKenney; Vjekoslav Nemesh's collection of hand-painted glass vessels; Ron van de Vlugt of de Flute's hand-blown glass vases and dishes; David Trubridge's lightshades.
Exhibition schedule: Refer to the gallery website for current and future exhibitions.
Artists represented: Artworks: Timo Rannali, Kate Jones Madill, Rebecca Meyer, Nick Eggleston, Raymond Fowler, Rob McGregor, Tallulah Belle Lautrec-Nunes, Val Tubman, Sylvia Davidson, Colleen Dewhurst, Grant Simpson, Lynne Mathieson, Vjekoslav Nemesh, Phillip Krammer, Heidi Borchardt, Sharen Watson, Heather Wilson. Sculptors: Brett Taylor, John Wolter, Janene Sullivan, Tui Slater, James Atutahi, Nick Clegg. Glass artisans: Ron van de Vlugt, Jason Svendsen, Vjekoslav Nemesh, Jan Kocian, Lynden Over.
Where to eat: Zambezi Licensed Café is recommended.
What else to do nearby: Shop at the Mount's Main Street shopping precinct; walk around and up the Mount and along either the beach or Pilot Bay.

Gisborne/Hawke's Bay

Artmosphere Gallery (D)

Address: 92 Vogel Street, Woodville
Phone number: (06) 376 4300
Website: www.artmosphere-gallery.com
Gallery Directors: Sally Maguire and Helmut Hirler
Building: Old Post Office Hotel on SH2

Opening times: 10 am to 5 pm daily (summer); 10 am to 5 pm Thursday to Monday (winter).
Admission charges: Free
Guided tours: On request
Wheelchair access: Yes
Toilets: Yes

Artmosphere Gallery features some of the finest artists in New Zealand, including Helmut Hirler, a world-renowned photographer from Germany, landscape oil artist Don Hill and glass artist Katie Brown. The gallery displays a wide variety of paintings, as well as a selection of jewellery, sculpture and fine art photography.

Artmosphere Gallery

Collection: The gallery's collection includes a range of works.

Exhibition schedule: The gallery does not have a regular exhibition schedule.

Artists represented: Liane Ashman, Katie Brown, Jerome de Bouter, Di Conway, Janice and Teresa Corbishley, Kevin Dunkley, Gerard McCabe, Bill Davies, Robert Franken, Matt Guild, Don Hill, Helmut Hirler, Sue James, Joanne Kay, Nickee Kelly, Crispin Korschen, Jan Kerr, Sally Maguire, Campbell Maud, Adrian Moerenhout, Jacky Pearson, Gavan Riley, Kerk Taylor, Tracy Skelton, Marea Tuarau, Brendon Sole, Marc Vigor-Brown, Bodhi Vincent.

Where to eat: There are numerous cafés located in Woodville town.

What else to do nearby: Visit the wind turbines capital of New Zealand; hike though the Manawatu Gorge; get adventurous with a jetboat ride; or visit antique shops in the township.

Lindauer – The Woodville Connection

An artist who left a lasting legacy for New Zealand was Gottfried Lindauer, born 5 January 1839 in Plzen, Czech Republic. Lindauer started a gardening apprenticeship with his father in 1852 at age 13, and three years later he travelled to Vienna, Austria, to study art. During his training, Lindauer was called into the reserves of the Austrian Army. However, he was not deemed soldier material and ended up painting portraits of the officers' wives. He was again called upon to serve in 1873 but after quarreling with the officers, he took a year's leave of absence and boarded the first ship departing Hamburg on 10 May 1874. He arrived in Wellington, New Zealand on 6 August. Leading a somewhat nomadic life, he travelled regularly through the country with Dr Walter Buller, attending Maori Land Courts and painting portraits of judges and solicitors. His first known painting in New Zealand was of Sir Ernest Davis' mother in 1875.

Lindauer painted a wide variety of subject matter, including portraits of settlers, but he became fascinated with painting Maori and their way of life. In late 1875, or early 1876, he shifted to Auckland, where he met Henry Partridge, a local businessman who was to become his chief patron. There was widespread feeling at this time that the Maori race was dying out and Partridge believed that there was an urgent need for a pictorial record of traditional Maori. Over the next 30 or so years he commissioned from Lindauer many portraits and depictions of Maori life, which accurately record facial tattoos, clothing, ornaments and weapons. These paintings have grown in stature over the years and are now highly sought after by collectors, commanding premium prices at auction.

In 1889, Lindauer visited Woodville to purchase a section and the following year he secured a 10-acre block in Pinfold Road where he built his house and studio and grew grapes. A keen gardener, he spent a great deal of time landscaping and planting trees, many of which are still there.

The artist passed away in his sleep, as had been his wish, on 13 June 1926 at his Woodville home. He is buried in the Woodville Historic Gorge Cemetery.

Replica Studio: The Woodville District Vision Committee erected a replica studio in June 2001. It contains furniture and reproductions of Gottfried Lindauer's work. The studio is situated in Vogel Street, the main street of Woodville, alongside the Tararua Visitor Information Centre. Viewing is by entry through the Tararua i-SITE.

Hastings City Art Gallery (P)

Address: *Civic Square, 201 Eastbourne Street East, Hastings*
Phone number: *(06) 871 5095*
Website: *www.hastingscityartgallery.co.nz*
Gallery Director: *Maree Mills*
Building: *1970s single-storey architectural gem.*

Opening times: *10 am to 4.30 pm daily.*
Admission charges: *Free*
Guided tours: *By appointment, please contact the gallery for more information.*
Wheelchair access: *Yes*
Toilets: *Yes*

Hastings City Art Gallery aims to bring together art that excites, challenges and extends cultural experiences and connects with people, place and identity. Exhibiting top quality, broad-ranging national and international artworks and promoting the work of renowned regional artists, the Hastings City Art Gallery is a stunning space to visit and enjoy. With three exhibition spaces it provides the local community and visitors with an engaging and varied exhibition schedule. Public programmes are designed for specific exhibitions. Situated in the city's Civic Square, the gallery is a short walk from the central city and next to the Hastings Library. Hastings City Art Gallery also has a retail area stocking quirky jewellery and a unique range of cards and art books. Entry is free and the gallery welcomes large and small groups.

Collection: The gallery does not have a permanent collection.
Exhibition schedule: Wide range of exhibitions, both touring and curated in-house. Refer to the gallery website for current and future exhibitions.
Artists represented: The gallery does not represent individual artists.
Where to eat: Try The Opera Kitchen (corner of Eastbourne and Hastings Streets), Café at Westerman's (Russell Street), Taste Cornucopia Organic Café (Heretaunga Street) and many other eateries in and around the locality.
What else to do nearby: Visit Hastings Community Art Centre, the Hawke's Bay Opera House and Hastings Library; see a movie at Reading Cinemas and shop in the central city.

Hovding Gallery (D)

Address: 6 Hovding Street, Lower Norsewood
Phone number: (06) 374 0897
Website: www.nznaturalclothing.co.nz
Gallery Director: Phil Grant
Building: Formerly an historic post office, dairy factory merchandise store and the offices of Norsewear.

Opening times: 9 am to 5 pm daily.
Admission charges: Free
Guided tours: Tours can be conducted through the Norsewear Sock Factory by appointment.
Wheelchair access: Yes
Toilets: Yes

This gallery is named after one of the Scandinavian settlers' vessels and is in its infant stages. It displays a wide range of local art and includes oils, watercolours, native timber carvings, acrylics on saws and canvas, pottery, photography and woodturning. The gallery is a low-commission service to the community and is housed in the former Norsewear boardroom adjacent to the iconic clothing store of 43 years. The building was formerly a post office in the 1800s and from the 1920s it was a dairy factory merchandise store. Many heritage pieces are on display along with historical information on the way things were and interesting stories from the local region. Complimentary filter coffee, tea and water are available. Hovding Gallery is located 1 hour's drive from Palmerston North and Napier.

Collection: Hovding Gallery has a collection of heritage pieces from the region.
Exhibition schedule: The gallery does not have a regular exhibition schedule.
Artists represented: Elinor Hughes, Gill Charmley, Maurice Brookes, Brenda Blackett, Mike Harold, Jacquie Anderson, Jeff Bryan and many more.
Where to eat: Try Café Norsewood, Norsewood Crown Hotel and Matamau Diner.
What else to do nearby: Visit the Norsewood Pioneer Museum; play a round at the Norsewood Golf Club; buy Dutch products at Scandi Superette; enroll for a cheesemaking course at Rangiuru Goat Farm; take the Troll Stroll heritage walk; let the children play on the flying fox in the playground across from the gallery.

Kahukura Gallery (D)

Address: 34 Ormond Road, Gisborne
Phone number: (06) 868 0970
Website: The gallery does not have a website
Gallery Director: Ngaroimata Winiata
Building: Private residence
Opening times: 10 am to 4 pm Saturday and

Sunday; Monday to Friday by appointment.
Admission charges: $2
Guided tours: Yes
Wheelchair access: Yes
Toilets: Yes

Kahukura Gallery is a contemporary art gallery and project space specialising in traditional and contemporary Maori and Pacific art from Aotearoa New Zealand and the Pacific. Kahukura is a gallery that supports local and national emerging and recognised artists. It has a gallery and workspace where people are invited to participate in workshops with art practitioners from throughout Aotearoa. Kahukura Gallery offers a unique cultural experience.

Collection: Tame Iti, John Miller, Mark Kopua.
Exhibition schedule: The gallery does not have an exhibition schedule.
Artists represented: Phil Mokaraka Berry, Tania Miller (Australia), Tattane Koia, Bernise Williams, Cherie Te Rore, Denise Christie Beale.
Where to eat: There are cafés within walking distance.
What else to do nearby: Visit local museums and the rose gardens; riverside walks and beaches all within walking distance.

McHardy Street Gallery (A)

Address: 6 McHardy Street, Havelock North
Phone number: (06) 877 4642 or 027 373 8113
Website: www.creativehawkesbay.co.nz
Gallery Director: Gina Guerin
Building: 1920s renovated villa
Opening times: 2 pm to 5 pm Thursday to Sunday (summer); 2 pm to 5 pm Saturdays (winter). Look for open sign displayed at gate.
Admission charges: Free
Guided tours: Art demonstrations can be arranged for small groups.
Wheelchair access: No
Toilets: Yes

Set in lovely cottage gardens, this new gallery is part of a renovated 1920s villa. Only minutes from Havelock North village, the gallery shows Gina Guerin's latest vibrant acrylic landscapes and abstracts with New Zealand elements. A new series of round paintings feature a glossy resin finish.

Collection: Collection of semi-abstract paintings featuring nudes, landscapes, still life and stylised faces. The works range from large canvases to smaller works on paper, which are mounted and shrink-wrapped, ready to frame. There is also a selection of art cards featuring the artist's colourful images.
Exhibition schedule: Works change regularly as new series are exhibited.
Artist represented: Gina Guerin
Where to eat: There are many cafés nearby in Havelock North village.
What else to do nearby: There are several wineries nearby and a cheese factory at the end of Te Mata Road. Also in the same area is the Black Barn Vineyards, art gallery and restaurant. Havelock North is 20 minutes by car from local beaches and the art deco city of Napier.

Paper-Works Gallery (D)

Address: *Upstairs, 27 Tennyson Street, Napier*
Phone number: *(06) 835 3859*
Website: *www.paper-works.co.nz*
Gallery Director: *Annabel Sinclair-Thomson*
Building: *Art deco building*
Opening times: *10 am to 4 pm Monday to*
Saturday (summer); closed Tuesday and
Wednesday during winter.
Admission charges: *Free*
Guided tours: *No*
Wheelchair access: *No*
Toilets: *Yes*

Based in the heart of Napier is a secret art haven representing over 60 artists and bringing together works from established artists and those who are on their way. Paper-Works deals mainly with works on paper, allowing the gallery to stock a much wider variety of works that appeal to different tastes and budgets. The works range from paintings, pencil drawings, watercolours, original limited edition prints (e.g. engravings, etchings, mezzotints and lithographs), photographs and more. Art books and other art related items are also for sale. Paper-Works Gallery attracts both the serious collector and those who are just starting their love affair with art, their affordability never detracting from their ability to delight or their investment potential.

Collection: The gallery does not have a permanent collection.
Exhibition schedule: Occasional exhibitions
Artists represented: Lex Benson-Cooper, Grant Beran, Sam Broad, Michele Bryant, Nigel Buxton, Gavin Chilcott, Matthew Couper, Brian and Leane Culy, Tony de Lautour, John Drawbridge, Fane Flaws, Dick Frizzell, Michael Hawksworth, Maree Horner, Scott Kennedy, Marian Maguire, Piera McArthur, Sara McIntyre, Martin Poppelwell, Don Ramage, Kahu Scott, Margaret Silverwood, Basia Smolnicki, Eion Stevens, Michel Tuffery, Gary Waldrom.
Where to eat: There are numerous cafés and restaurants nearby.
What else to do nearby: Visit Hawke's Bay Museum and Art Gallery.

Paul Nache (D)

Address: *Upstairs, 89 Grey Street, Gisborne*
Phone number: *(06) 867 9721*
Website: *www.paulnache.com*
Gallery Director: *Matthew Nache*
Building: *Historic building located on the*
corner of Gladstone Road and Grey Street
in central Gisborne.
Opening times: *10 am to 5 pm Wednesday*
to Friday; 10 am to 2 pm Saturday.
Admission charges: *Free*
Guided tours: *Yes*
Wheelchair access: *No*
Toilets: *Yes*

Paul Nache Gallery is dedicated to exhibiting work by contemporary artists. The gallery has been defying convention since it opened more than 6 years ago, favouring their historic inner-city Gisborne location over the country's main centres. Paul Nache specialises in the sale of significant works of contemporary art.

Collection: The gallery does not have a permanent collection.
Exhibition schedule: The gallery hosts frequent solo and curated exhibitions usually on the first Friday of every month.
Artists represented: Peter Adsett, Valerie Bos, Mark Braunias, Matthew Couper, Steve Gibbs, Star Gossage, Dion Hitchens, Rob Hood, Robert Jahnke, Joanna Langford, Robert McLeod, James Ormsby, Ben Pearce, Bill Riley, James Robinson, Jack Straker, William Suttle, Sanjay Theodore, Geoff Tune, Johnny Turner and John Walsh.
Where to eat: Downstairs on Grey Street is locally owned fresh Japanese sushi, The Winemakers Daughters with superior coffee, local pie shop and bakery, Turkish kebabs, pizza, numerous restaurants and wine bars.
What else to do nearby: Visit Tairawhiti Gisborne Museum and Art Gallery; enjoy Cellar Door wine tastings; walk around amazing local rivers and beaches. The historic landing site of Captain James Cook's first encounter with indigenous Maori on Kaiti Hill is approximately 5 minutes' walking distance from the gallery.

Quay Gallery (D)

Address: 14 West Quay, Ahuriri, Napier
Phone number: (06) 835 4637
Website: www.quaygallery.co.nz
Gallery Director: Richard Meyers
Building: Street level of a recently developed residential apartment complex.
Opening times: 10 am to 5 pm Monday to
Saturday; 10 am to 4 pm Sunday.
Admission charges: Free
Guided tours: Yes, tours undertaken by the gallery director.
Wheelchair access: Yes
Toilets: Yes

Quay Gallery was opened on 1 January 2008 by Sue Schaare and Richard Meyers, on a waterfront setting among cafés, restaurants and new apartments and with fishing boats moored close by. The gallery is only minutes from the centre of Napier. It offers fine viewing for all contemporary and traditional art lovers with regular solo and group shows. Among the exhibits are original authentic paintings, sculptures, ceramics, glass, bronze and jewellery all created by New Zealand artists. Quay Gallery offers a relaxed atmosphere in which to browse through books on art or view the artists at work in their studios via DVD television. The gallery represents many of Hawke's Bay emerging artists as well as established New Zealand artists. They stock over 200 paintings and prints covering landscape and seascape, contemporary, traditional and abstract works.

Quay Gallery

Collection: Investment art: Gary Waldrom; David Traub (Glass Artist of the Year 2008); NgAng (Pastel Artist of the Year 2008); Sue Hawker (glass artist, winner of the Ranamok Glass Exhibition Canberra 2010); Jaymz Edmonds (glass artist, finalist of the Ranamok Glass Exhibition Canberra 2008); John Lawrence (ceramic artist); and Anne Verdcourt (ceramic artist).

Exhibition schedule: Up to eight solo or group exhibitions held per year except for the months of February, March, June and July. Refer to the gallery website for current and future exhibitions.

Artists represented: Painters: Gary Waldrom, Anna Stitchbury, Sue Schaare, Ross Lee, Michelle Bellamy, Russell Jackson, Jane Puckey, Belinda Wilson, Ernest Papps, NgAng, Julie Greig, John Spittle, John Staniford, Ken Nysse, Nicola Forster. Glass artists: David Traub, Sue Hawker, Jaymz Edmonds, Justine Culina, Joanne Kay Cosford, Brendon Sole. Ceramic artists: John Lawrence, Ann Verdcourt, Brian Gartside. Bronze artists: Jo Barwick, Roddy McMillan. Sculptor: Kap Pothan.

Where to eat: There are cafés and restaurants next door and several within 200 metres.

What else to do nearby: Wander around the waterfront boardwalk at Ahuriri village; visit antique shops and craft galleries; take fishing and boat trips. Napier is famous for its art deco heritage buildings and guided tours are available. Or, take an adventure tour to view the gannet colony at Cape Kidnappers.

Red Peach Gallery (D)

Address: Cnr Waghorne and Bridge Streets, Ahuriri, Napier
Phone number: (06) 835 4773 or 027 388 5763
Website: www.redpeachgallery.com
Gallery Director: Janice Corbishley
Building: Masonry building in a block of vibrant retail outlets and apartments

Opening times: 10 am to 4 pm Tuesday to Saturday; 11 am to 4 pm Sunday.
Admission charges: Free
Guided tours: No
Wheelchair access: Yes
Toilets: No

Situated in the idyllic seaside village of Ahuriri in Napier, the Red Peach Gallery exhibits quality paintings, glass, ceramics and jewellery by Hawke's Bay and New Zealand artists. A varied selection of interesting art, friendly staff and the intimacy of the gallery create an atmosphere which leaves most visitors singing its praises and promising to return. Red Peach Gallery is owned by well-known mosaic artist Janice Corbishley.

Collection: Ion Brown, Michael Blow, Don Hill, Ben Ho, Piera McArthur, Lance O'Gorman, Pauline O'Sullivan, Jacky Pearson, Brent Redding, Des Robertshaw, John Staniford, Brian Strong, Wayne Sinclair, Peter Wallers.

Exhibition schedule: Refer to the gallery website for current and future exhibitions.

Artists represented: Graham Ambrose, Robyn Barclay, Brian Barnhill, Andrea Beech, Helena Blair, Chris Bone, Deb Bell, Jos Coufreur, Fiona Gedson, Glenda Gibbs, Raewyn Harris, Nicholas Hayter, Jennifer Heath, Lou Pendergrast-Mathieson, Kim Morgan, Katherine Quinn, Ron

Reichs, Hugh Ricard, Megan Schmidt, Nic Scotland, Daniel Smith, Kathie Sumpter, Marc Vigor-Brown, Peter Wallers.

Where to eat: There is a great selection of cafés and restaurants, including Thai, Indian, Japanese sushi, Italian, bistro, fine dining and seaside bars.

What else to do nearby: Browse the antique shops and galleries; take fishing, boating trips; walk the boardwalk by the seaside or go swimming. Napier is famous for its art deco heritage buildings and guided tours are available. Take an adventure tour to view the gannet colony at Cape Kidnappers.

Tairawhiti Museum and Art Gallery (P)

Address: 10 Stout Street, Gisborne
Phone number: (06) 867 3832
Website: www.tairawhitimuseum.org.nz
Gallery Director: Dr David Butts
Building: Purpose built in 1977
Opening times: 10 am to 4 pm Monday to Saturday; 1.30 pm to 4 pm Sunday and public holidays; closed Easter Friday, Christmas Day and Boxing Day.
Admission charges: Residents and ratepayers of Gisborne $2; visitors $5.
Guided tours: On request
Wheelchair access: Yes
Toilets: Yes

Tairawhiti Museum and Art Gallery is a regional institution providing a programme of exhibitions by local artists and travelling exhibitions from other galleries. The museum has a significant regional art collection, focusing in particular on East Coast landscapes, customary and contemporary Maori art from Tairawhiti and an excellent representation of artists who have lived and worked in Tairawhiti.

Collection: Significant artists and works: John Hovell (Painting: *East Cape Garden ii: Awakening upon hearing the first cuckoo, I whea koe I te tanghanga o te pipiwharauroa*), Derek Lardelli (Sculpture: *Te Uhi*, 1998), Robert Jahnke (Sculpture), Baye Riddell (Ceramic works), Geoff Tune (Painting: *East Coast Landscape*, 1968).

Exhibition schedule: Refer to the gallery website for current and future exhibitions.

Artists represented: The gallery does not represent individual artists.

Where to eat: Exhibit Café is located on-site.

What else to do nearby: Follow the Turanganui Heritage Precinct walk; visit Cook National Memorial celebrating Cook's first landing in New Zealand in 1769; also the Paul Nache gallery is nearby in the city.

Taranaki /Manawatu

Govett-Brewster Art Gallery (P)

Address: *42 Queen Street, New Plymouth*
Phone number: *(06) 759 6060*
Website: *www.govettbrewster.com*
Gallery Director: *Rhana Devenport*
Opening times: *10 am to 5 pm daily.*
Closed Christmas Day.
Admission charges: *Free, donations welcome.*
Guided tours: *Public events in the Govett-Brewster, which often incorporate tours of a specific location, are held every Sunday. Groups can book a private guided tour by contacting the gallery.*
Wheelchair access: *A parking space for mobility-impaired visitors, wheelchair hire and full wheelchair access to Govett-Brewster spaces are provided. Contact the gallery prior to your visit to book a wheelchair.*
Toilets: *Yes*

The Govett-Brewster Art Gallery, established in 1970, is Aotearoa New Zealand's premier contemporary art museum. The Govett-Brewster seeks to offer a responsive, accessible, relevant, dynamic and stimulating hub for an open exchange of ideas and engagements with the art and cultures of today – thus nurturing innovation, research, creativity and dialogue for people from all walks of life. The gallery is recognised nationally and internationally for its global vision, its special commitment to art from the Pacific, and as home to the art and ideas of pioneering filmmaker and kinetic artist, Len Lye. Exhibitions curated by the Govett-Brewster have toured New Zealand and international art museums. Works from the Govett-Brewster's permanent collection have also been loaned to other art and cultural institutions.

Collection: The gallery holds a small but significant collection of contemporary artwork that is continually expanding.
Exhibition schedule: The gallery aims to present a dynamic and groundbreaking exhibition programme to gallery audiences. The Govett-Brewster presents over 10 exhibitions every year, showcasing the best of local, national and international contemporary art. Refer to the gallery website for current and future exhibitions.
Artists represented: The gallery does not represent individual artists.
Where to eat: Café Govett-Brewster located next to the Art & Design Shop in the foyer of the gallery is open daily.
What else to do nearby: Visit the Todd Energy Aquatic Centre or Puke Ariki – and learn about the history of Taranaki; walk around Pukekura Park.

Sarjeant Gallery (P)

Address: Queens Park, Whanganui
Phone number: (06) 349 0506
Website: www.sarjeant.org.nz
Senior Curator: Greg Anderson
Building: In 1915 the Wanganui Borough Council and its Mayor C. E. Mackay appointed Samuel Hurst Seager, a distinguished Christchurch architect and lecturer at the Canterbury College School of Art, as assessor for a competition to select a design for the gallery. Donald Hosie, the articled pupil of Dunedin-based architect Edmund Anscombe, was announced the winner in 1916. Building commenced in May 1917 and the gallery was officially opened by Prime Minister William Massey on 6 September 1919. The Sarjeant Gallery has a New Zealand Historic Places Trust Category I listing.

Opening times: 10.30 am to 4.30 pm Monday to Sunday; 1.30 pm to 4.30 pm Anzac Day. Closed Good Friday and Christmas Day.
Admission charges: Free
Guided tours: By appointment
Wheelchair access: Yes
Toilets: Yes

On his death in 1912, prominent local businessman Henry Sarjeant left a bequest for the establishment of 'a Fine Arts Gallery for the reception, purchase and acquisition of pictures and sculpture and other works of art for the public benefit and for the use of the public'. The magnificent Sarjeant Gallery is one of New Zealand's finest and most historically important public art galleries. The Sarjeant is renowned for its neoclassical architecture, natural lighting and magnificent display spaces, with its distinctive Greek cross shape, 13-metre high central dome and exquisite architectural detailing greatly enhancing the visitor experience. The gallery has a permanent collection of over 5500 artworks, including an extensive collection of early 19th- and 20th-century British and European works and a large collection of contemporary New Zealand art, which is often drawn from and displayed within a dynamic, diverse and regularly changing exhibition programme. This is a much sought-after resource often loaned out to other institutions. From these and other artworks, the Sarjeant Gallery also generates touring exhibitions. The gallery shop specialises in contemporary jewellery and glass, stocks exhibition catalogues and a wide range of cards.

Sarjeant Gallery

Collection: Given the terms of Henry Sarjeant's will, the initial primary collection focus on early British and European art has resulted in an international collection of works that rank as the most notable in New Zealand outside the four main centres. The emphasis of this part of the collection is on late 19th-century English painting and it includes two works by the Pre-Raphaelite Sir Edward Burne-Jones. Of note also are the collection of drawings of the Stations of the Cross from the studio of Bernadino Poccetti (1540s–1612) and an extensive collection of World War I cartoons.

Work by New Zealand artists was first acquired in 1926 and increasingly has become the primary collecting focus. This collection is a significant and comprehensive holding of art from the 1840s until the present day and contains works by two of the region's nationally recognised artists, J. A. Gilfillan and Edith Marion Collier. Over the past 25 years the Sarjeant has demonstrated a strong commitment to contemporary photography, building on its important early Frank Denton photographic collection with works by Laurence Aberhart, Peter Peryer, Anne Noble, Ans Westra, Wayne Barrar, Yvonne Todd, Megan Jenkinson, Ed Ruscha and George Krause.

Exhibition schedule: The gallery schedules its exhibition programme on a quarterly basis with approximately 22 exhibitions a year. These are accompanied by a lively series of public talks and events.

Artists represented: Domenico Piola, Sir Frank Brangwyn RA, Gaspard Dughet, Sir William Richmond RA, William Etty, Lelio Orsi, Frederick Goodall RA, Augustus John RA, Eugen von Blaas, Rosa Bonheur, Colin McCahon, Ralph Hotere, Frances Hodgkins, Charles F. Goldie, Gottfried Lindauer, Petrus van der Velden, Gordon Walters, Gretchen Albrecht, Pat Hanly, Philip Trusttum, Robert McLeod, Warren Viscoe and Rodney Fumpston, Mervyn Williams, Milan Mrkusich.

Where to eat: Gallery staff will provide a list of cafés to enjoy.

What else to do nearby: Also in Queen's Park is the Whanganui Regional Museum, the Davis Central City Library, the Whanganui War Memorial Conference and Convention Centre and the Handspan Peace Sculpture. Nearby are Chronicle Glass Studio and Gallery, the Quay Gallery and the McNamara Gallery. Visit the historic Durie Hill Elevator or Whanganui Riverboat Centre to take a Waimarie Paddle Steamer tour.

Taylor Jensen Fine Arts (D)

Address: 33 George Street, Palmerston North
Phone number: (06) 355 4278
Website: www.finearts.co.nz
Gallery Director: Stuart Schwartz
Building: Norfolk House, a 1925 two-storey building.
Opening times: 10 am to 5 pm Monday to Thursday; 10 am to 6 pm Friday; 10 am to 3 pm Saturday.
Admission charges: Free
Guided tours: By appointment
Wheelchair access: No
Toilets: Staff toilet available upon request. Public toilets next door at the Palmerston North City Library.

Taylor Jensen Fine Arts was established in 1997 to showcase the work of local artists and artisans. This premier art gallery offers the best in local and regional New Zealand art in all media, oil and acrylic paintings, watercolours, graphics, sculpture, glass, ceramics, turned and carved wood, textiles, jewellery, furniture and design, Maori art and more. It is located in the 'arty' Westside of Palmerston North and features a 65-square-metre changing exhibition space where 12 to 15 group or solo exhibitions are shown annually. As a 'community gallery', space is often given over to arts organisations for annual exhibitions or competitions. Among over 125 artists who have shown their work at Taylor Jensen Fine Arts are internationally recognised sculptor Paul Dibble and portraitist Philip Holmes, as well as regional favourites like Jack Register, Vonnie Sterritt, Ernest Papps, Judy Johnstone, Brent Redding and Adele Souster. The retail section of the gallery is a treasure trove of mostly one-off artworks, original prints and graphics. It is also known as a great source for cards depicting original New Zealand art and themes.

Collection: As a privately owned dealer gallery, Taylor Jensen Fine Arts sells on behalf and owns only a few works which continue to be listed as inventory of the gallery.
Exhibition schedule: Changing exhibitions installed monthly. Refer to the gallery website for current and future exhibitions.

Taylor Jensen Fine Arts

Artists represented: Painters: Brent Redding, Adele Souster, Judy Johnstone, Jack Register, Ross Whitlock, Fran Dibble, Vonnie Sterritt, Alan Wehipeihana, Jane Ross, Miki Clarke, David Taylor, Wei Wu. Sculptors: Paul Dibble, the late Rik Land, Bill Hayes, Olivier Duhamel, Steuart Welch. Ceramists: Kim Morgan, Trevor Wright, Wilma Jennings, Stephanie Cahorel. Glass Blowers: Lynden Over, Jan Kocian, Ron van der Vlugt. Jewellers: Melanie Mills, Ruth Taylor, Isla Osborne. Woodturners: Dick Patston, Robert McCallum, Graham Baker, John Wysocki, John Bramley, Roy Miers, Jim Neumann. Furniture Makers: Andy Halewood, Josh Norris, Martin Carryer.
Where to eat: See a wide variety of eating establishments on George Street: Kuppa Café (inside the library), Barista, Trio Café, Alexandre Patisserie, Café 40, Café Jacko, Mao Bar, Moxies, Mr India, Indian2nite.
What else to do nearby: Visit Te Manawa Museum of Art, Science and History, the Palmerston North City Library, Zimmerman Contemporary Art Gallery and Thermostat Art Gallery. Use the *Arts Trail Guide* to enjoy public art in Palmerston North (available at gallery).

Wairarapa

Aratoi – Wairarapa Museum of Art and History (P)

Address: *Cnr Bruce and Dixon Streets, Masterton*
Phone number: *(06) 370 0001*
Website: *www.aratoi.org.nz*
Gallery Director: *Marcus Boroughs*
Building: *Aratoi evolved from the Wairarapa Arts Centre, which opened in 1969 on a site opposite its current location. The new building, dating from the 1990s, has a modern collection store that enables the facility to collect and display taonga, natural objects and artworks.*
Opening times: *10 am to 4 pm daily. Closed Good Friday, Christmas Day, Boxing Day and New Year's Day.*
Admission charges: *Gold coin donation*
Guided tours: *'Behind the Scenes Tour' by appointment only.*
Wheelchair access: *Yes*
Toilets: *Yes*

Aratoi is a modern museum and gallery in Masterton offering a rich and varied experience of contemporary New Zealand art and craft. It is home to a number of important collections of New Zealand art and a collection of taonga (treasure) that tell the stories of the Wairarapa and its people.

Collection: Aratoi is committed to representing Wairarapa artists. It is home to a number of important collections, including the Prior Collection and the Rutherford Trust Collection, which feature works by Colin McCahon, Rita Angus, Ralph Hotere and Sir Toss Wollaston. Donations, bequests and friends initiatives enable Aratoi to continue making new acquisitions. Aratoi acts as kaitiaki (guardian) to a growing collection of Maori taonga, historic and natural objects.

Exhibition schedule: Refer to the gallery website for current and future exhibitions.

Artists represented: Recent exhibitions have featured high profile Wairarapa artists such as Robin White, Gavin Chilcott, Brendon Wilkinson, Kate Small, Rhondda Greig, Kirsty Gardiner, Megan Campbell, Janet Green, Harry Watson.

Where to eat: Entice Café next door has great coffee and delicious food.

What else to do nearby: Queen Elizabeth Park is directly across the road. See Shear Discovery for The Wool Shed – The National Museum of Sheep and Shearing. Visit the Masterton Information Centre for more information. Greytown offers great shopping and wineries and is a short 15-minute drive away.

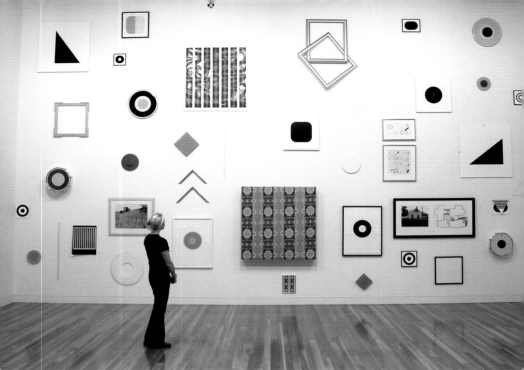

Aratoi – Wairarapa Museum of Art and History

Colours For Art (D)

Address: 444 Queen Street, Kuripuni, Masterton
Phone number: (06) 377 5844
Website: www.coloursforart.co.nz
Gallery Director: Jim Campbell
Opening times: 10 am to 5 pm Monday to Friday; 10 am to 3 pm Saturday.
Admission charges: Free
Guided tours: No
Wheelchair access: Yes
Toilets: Yes

Colours For Art not only has a number of local artists' work but also has supplies for the artist from watercolour paint and paper to acrylics, brushes and mediums. There is art hanging in the shop and the back gallery has individual artists exhibiting their work. The gallery also specialises in framing and has a huge range of frames available. They can also digitally enhance your photographs for printing on canvas or block mounted to create stunning pieces of ready-to-hang art.

Collection: The gallery does not have a permanent collection.
Exhibition schedule: The gallery does not hold exhibitions.
Artists represented: Jim Campbell, Anna-Marie Kingsley, David Knowles, Jane Sinclair, Paul Martinson, Annette Dunnage-Roy, Jacky Pearson, Marion Long.
Where to eat: There are local cafés nearby.
What else to do nearby: Stroll around Kuripuni village.

Mark Dimock Gallery (A)

Address: 87 High Street, Eketahuna
Phone number: (06) 375 8213
Website: www.markdimock.co.nz
Gallery Director: Mark Dimock
Building: Adjacent to the artist's residence
Opening times: Daylight hours whenever the artist is home.
Admission charges: Free
Guided tours: The artist is available to assist visitors at all times.
Wheelchair access: Yes
Toilets: Yes

The Mark Dimock Gallery is a signature gallery with all work on display being created by the artist. It is situated on the edge of the small town of Eketahuna in northern Wairarapa. Mark's works are contemporary sculpture and painting incorporating aluminium, steel, timber and paint, often together.

Collection: A large collection of works covering the artist's career from 1975 to the present day.
Exhibition schedule: The gallery does not hold exhibitions.
Artist represented: Mark Dimock
Where to eat: There are eateries in Eketahuna township.
What else to do nearby: Visit Pukaha Mount Bruce National Wildlife Centre; tramping or walks in the Tararua Ranges.

Red Barn Art (A)

Address: 65 White Rock Road, Martinborough
Phone number: (06) 306 6161
Website: www.redbarnart.co.nz
Gallery Director: Matt Guild
Building: Adjacent to the artist's residence
Opening times: Daylight hours whenever the artist is home.
Admission charges: Free
Guided tours: On request
Wheelchair access: Yes
Toilets: Yes

Red Barn Art is the working studio gallery of resident artist Matt Guild. Matt works in the studio and displays his latest paintings in the gallery. He works with realistic, still life images that capture the emotional history of New Zealand. He takes ordinary, often seemingly mundane or everyday objects and injects these familiar forms with new emotional life by positioning them in the more whimsical landscape of our memories. His paintings are about light, shadow and reflections, and about the way things look in their environment.

Collection: Matt Guild
Exhibition schedule: New works displayed and available all year round.
Artists represented: Matt Guild painter, local artist in residence; Doug Kennedy, sculptor.
Where to eat: There are many good local cafés in Martinborough.
What else to do nearby: Winery tours and fantastic cafés in the locality.

Wellington

Bowen Galleries (D)

Address: 39 Ghuznee Street, Wellington
Phone number: (04) 381 0351
Website: www.bowengalleries.co.nz
Gallery Directors: Penney Moir and
Jenny Neligan
Opening times: 10 am to 5.30 pm Monday
to Friday; 10 am to 3 pm Saturday.
Admission charges: Free
Guided tours: No
Wheelchair access: Yes
Toilets: No

Bowen Galleries represents New Zealand and Australian contemporary artists, many of them in public gallery collections and major private collections.

Bowen Galleries

Collection: Bowen Galleries do not have permanent collections.
Exhibition schedule: Refer to the gallery website for current and future exhibitions.
Artists represented: Refer to the gallery website for a list of artists.
Where to eat: Milk Crate and Customs Brew Bar are both on Ghuznee Street.
What else to do nearby: Shop at Quilters Bookshop next door to gallery; visit the New Zealand Film Archive, a short distance down the road; stroll around Cuba Mall and explore the five other dealer galleries nearby.

City Gallery Wellington (P)

Address: Civic Square, 101 Wakefield Street, Wellington
Phone number: (04) 801 3021
Website: www.citygallery.org.nz
Gallery Director: Paula Savage
Building: In 1993 the gallery moved to its present location on the north-eastern side of Civic Square. Built in 1940 in an art deco style,

the gallery's current building originally housed the Wellington Public Library.
Opening times: 10 am to 5 pm daily.
Admission charges: Free, charges may apply for some shows.
Guided tours: By appointment
Wheelchair access: Yes
Toilets: Yes

Spectacularly located in the heart of Civic Square, City Gallery Wellington offers distinctive, memorable exhibitions of contemporary New Zealand and international art. The gallery provides visitors with sometimes challenging, always captivating, art from some of the world's most exciting artists. With two dedicated galleries showing the work of Wellington, Maori and Pacific artists, City Gallery Wellington enables diverse audiences to experience art in new and inspiring ways.

City Gallery Wellington

Collection: The gallery does not have a permanent collection.
Exhibition schedule: Refer to the gallery website for current and future exhibitions and events.
Artists represented: Refer to the gallery website for a list of artists.
Where to eat: Nikau Café is on the ground floor of the gallery.
What else to do nearby: Visit the Museum of Wellington City & Sea, Te Papa and Wellington Central Library.

Exhibitions Gallery of Fine Art (D)

Address: 154 Featherston Street
(cnr Featherston and Brandon Streets),
Wellington
Phone number: (04) 499 6356
Website: www.exhibitionsgallery.co.nz
Gallery Director: Ronald Epskamp
Opening times: 9.30 am to 5.30 pm Monday
to Friday; 11 am to 3 pm Saturday;
open Sunday in summer.
Admission charges: Free
Guided tours: No
Wheelchair access: Yes
Toilets: No

Exhibitions Gallery represents emerging artists alongside the more renowned, and exhibits and displays a range of works from representational and expressionist to abstract. There is a wide selection of landscapes, figurative works, sculpture and still life. As a gallery they continue to maintain and grow the quality, variety and range of the artworks for sale. If anything, the artwork is a personal reflection of gallery owner Ronald Epskamp's own diverse tastes in art and his insatiable appetite for discovering something different and exciting in the art arena. Exhibitions Gallery predominately features New Zealand artists and has a strong local contingent. In addition, they represent celebrated American pop artist Peter Mars, international artist Alison Coulthurst and they are also the agents for The Art of Dr Seuss. Whilst everyone may be familiar with Seuss' book illustrations, Seuss was foremost a visual artist who painted and sculpted for his own enjoyment. Exhibitions Gallery hosts The Art of Dr Seuss in roadshows throughout New Zealand. With monthly exhibitions the gallery continues to receive strong support from the people of Wellington and visitors to the capital.

Collection: The gallery does not have a permanent collection.
Exhibition schedule: Refer to the gallery website for current and future exhibitions.
Artists represented: Tony Allain, Rochelle Andrews, John Badcock, Allison Coulthurst, Di Conway, Lex Benson-Cooper, Kevin Dunkley, Gail Gauldie, Peter Hackett, Ben Ho, Daniella Hulme, Julian Knap, Rik Land, Catherine Manchester, Peter Mars, Ewan McDougall, Piera McArthur, Mark Olsen, Patterson Parkin, J. K. Reed, Dr Seuss, Colin Webster-Watson, Stephen Martyn Welch, Susan Webb, Geoff Williams.
Where to eat: There is a wide selection of quality eateries within a few minutes' walk.
What else to do nearby: Walk from Exhibitions Gallery along the waterfront to Te Papa, taking in many of Wellington's public sculptures along the way.

Kura Gallery (D)

Address: 19 Allen Street, Te Aro, Wellington
Phone number: (04) 802 4934
Website: www.kuragallery.co.nz
Gallery Director: Ben Dods
Opening times: 10 am to 6 pm Monday to
Friday; 11 am to 5 pm Saturday and Sunday.
Admission charges: Free
Guided tours: On request
Wheelchair access: Yes
Toilets: Yes

Kura Gallery invites you to step into a world of contemporary Maori and New Zealand art and design. The gallery features Maori carving, original artworks, innovative design, unique jewellery and genuine pounamu (greenstone or jade), all from Aotearoa New Zealand. Services include international delivery and printed material about the artists and artworks.

Collection: The gallery does not have a permanent collection.
Exhibition schedule: Bimonthly
Artists represented: Refer to the gallery website for a list of artists.
Where to eat: A large selection of cafés and restaurants can be found in the locality.
What else to do nearby: Visit Te Papa; enjoy the diverse retail shops in Courtenay Place.

McGregor Wright Gallery (D)

Address: 181 Raumati Road, Raumati, Kapiti Coast
Phone number: (04) 299 4958
Website: www.mcgregorwright.co.nz
Gallery Director: Gordon Cooksley
Opening times: 10 am to 5 pm Tuesday to
Saturday; 11 am to 4 pm Sunday.
Admission charges: Free
Guided tours: No
Wheelchair access: Please phone the gallery to arrange.
Toilets: No

This gallery was established in 1879 and has been operated by the present owners Nancye and Gordon Cooksley for the past 50 years. The gallery specialises in oils, watercolours and acrylics by top New Zealand artists from all over the country, especially impressionistic and realistic works which appeal to many people. Located 40 minutes from Wellington City on the Kapiti Coast it means there is plenty of parking at the door and the gallery has a relaxed home-like atmosphere inside and out. There is usually a display of around 100 or so paintings and a handful of bronzes, all carefully selected.

Collection: The gallery does not have a permanent collection.
Exhibition schedule: Changing on a regular basis. Refer to the gallery website for current and future exhibitions.
Artists represented: John Badcock, Brian Baxter, Michael Blow, Ion Brown, John Crump, Eugenea, Eva Hannah, Ben Ho, Tony Lewis, Michael Lubomudrov, Mary Mai, Alfred Memelink, Rob McDowell, Jacky Pearson, Anthony A. Prout, John Rundle.
Where to eat: There are numerous superb places to eat in the locality.

What else to do nearby: Visit the Kapiti Coast beaches; explore Kapiti Island Nature Reserve bird sanctuary; check out the Kapiti cheese factory and Waikanae village.

Millwood Gallery (D)

Address: 291B Tinakori Road, Thorndon
Phone number: (04) 473 5178
Website: www.millwoodgallery.co.nz
Gallery Director: Murray Pillar
Opening times: 9 am to 5.30 pm Monday to
Friday; 10 am to 4 pm Saturday;

11 am to 4 pm Sunday (December only).
Admission charges: Free
Guided tours: No
Wheelchair access: No
Toilets: No

Millwood Gallery can be found in the historic Tinakori Road village. Established in 1981, this gallery combines an extensive selection of paintings and original prints by contemporary New Zealand artists with carefully chosen books. A wide range of Wellington images is available. Author events and book groups are frequently hosted. Millwood Gallery is a place to spend time to find that special piece of art in unique, ambient surroundings.

Collection: The gallery does not have a permanent collection.
Exhibition schedule: Ongoing

Millwood Gallery

Artists represented: Philip Beadle, Roger Daniell, Janet de Wagt, Nic Dempster, Heather Dunckley, Carole Hughes, Robin Kay, Vivian Manthel-French, Philip Markham, Wendy Masters, Jane McIntosh, Pauline O'Sullivan, Tony Ogle, Margaret Palmer, Judith Royal, Annie Smits Sandano, Sue Schaare, Ted Sherwen, Susie Stone, Mary Taylor, Cynthia Taylor, Hilary Tipping, Judith Trevelyan, Gary Tricker, Roseanna Wohnsiedler.
Where to eat: There are cafés and restaurants nearby in the village.
What else to do nearby: Visit Tinakori Road village, the scenic Wellington Botanic Garden and Katherine Mansfield Birthplace Te Puakitanga.

Museum of New Zealand Te Papa Tongarewa (Te Papa) (P)

Address: Cable Street, Wellington
Phone number: (04) 381 7000
Website: www.tepapa.govt.nz
Chief Executive: Michael Houlihan, Michelle Hippolite (Kaihautū, or Maori leader)
Building: This striking building, designed by Jasmax Architects, received a mixed reception when it opened in 1998. The building's 'Maori face' overlooks the harbour while the 'European face' is oriented to the city. The wedge structure, which both unites and divides the two faces, houses the museum's Treaty of Waitangi exhibition.

Opening times: 10 am to 6 pm daily; 10 am to 9 pm Thursday, including public holidays.
Admission charges: Free, although charges apply to some short-term exhibitions and activities.
Guided tours: Te Papa offers daily tours for individuals and small groups. You can also hire an audio guide with information about selected exhibitions.
Wheelchair access: Yes, wheelchairs and a scooter are available. Good facilities for visitors with mobility impairment.
Toilets: Yes

Te Papa is New Zealand's national museum, renowned for being bicultural, scholarly, innovative and fun. The museum's success is built on its relationships with, and ability to represent, the community. Te Papa's collections span five areas: art, history, the Pacific, Maori and the natural environment. The exhibitions are interdisciplinary and interactive, and the museum hosts dynamic events and education programmes. Te Papa also has commercial enterprises including a publishing division, conference operations and retail stores.

Collection: Toi Te Papa Art of the Nation is a major celebration of New Zealand's rich and diverse artistic heritage. This long-term exhibition showcases hundreds of impressive artworks from Te Papa's collections. Iconic works from major artists like Heberley, Charles F. Goldie, Colin McCahon, Rita Angus, Ralph Hotere, Gretchen Albrecht and Shane Cotton sit alongside less well-known treasures, and recurring themes and art movements are explored.
Exhibition schedule: Refer to the museum website for current and future exhibitions.
Where to eat: Combine your visit to Te Papa with lunch, coffee and cake, or a glass of wine surrounded by our national treasures in one of the two cafés.
What else to do nearby: Enjoy the waterfront; walk over to City Gallery Wellington via the City to Sea Bridge; explore the galleries, music shops, boutiques and op shops of Cuba Mall.

New Zealand Academy of Fine Arts (P)

Address: *Wharf Office Apartments,*
1 Queens Wharf, Wellington
Phone number: *(04) 499 8807*
Website: *www.nzafa.com*
Gallery Director: *Justin Morgan*
Building: *In September 1998 the academy purchased three unit titles on the ground floor of the old Wellington Harbour Board offices at 1 Queens Wharf, on a 999-year lease. Herriot + Melhuish: Architecture Ltd designed*
and supervised the gallery fit out into three galleries. The facilities won three New Zealand Institute of Architects design awards in 2001 and this building is now known as the award-winning Wharf Office Apartments.
Opening times: *10 am to 5 pm daily.*
Admission charges: *Free*
Guided tours: *On request*
Wheelchair access: *Yes*
Toilets: *Yes*

New Zealand Academy of Fine Arts

The purpose of the New Zealand Academy of Fine Arts is to facilitate, nurture and develop the existing local and national art scene through the promotion, creation, understanding and enjoyment of all visual art forms. The academy has a proud 127-year history. It was founded in 1882 and between 1936 and 1970 the academy gifted its permanent collection of 426 paintings, which along with the Government's collection, created one national collection.

The academy functions as a non-profit organisation and is governed by a president and council of 12 who are unpaid and elected from the membership, which, alongside sales commissions and gallery hire, provides the academy with an income. In late 2010, the academy appointed a new director, gallery coordinator and office manager; and alongside these three people, rostered volunteers staff the gallery.

Collection: The New Zealand Academy of Fine Arts was largely set up in 1882 to provide a vehicle for a national art collection. In the years to 1967 over 500 works of art were gifted to the nation. Periodically during the intervening years the academy has collected works again to form the basis of a new collection. This is currently quite a small collection containing around 100 works. To date it represents a wide range of artists who have been involved with the academy since the 1970s, and with a few earlier pieces.

Exhibition schedule: The gallery hosts up to 10 hired shows throughout the year, which present a wide range of works from New Zealand and abroad, including one national or international touring show a year. Alongside these shows the academy hosts the following:

- Summer Tribute Exhibition, presenting work from a long-standing academy member
- Wellington's Dealer Art Fair, held biannually alongside the International New Zealand Art Festival
- Four academy member-based seasonal shows presenting over 150 pieces of work from throughout New Zealand
- Solo series: this happens twice a year with each show presenting works from 10 selected academy artists.

Refer to the gallery website for current and future exhibitions.

Artists represented: Over 400 New Zealand emerging and established artists.

Where to eat: Try Mojo Coffee and Foxglove Bar & Kitchen.

What else to do nearby: Visit the Museum of Wellington City & Sea, the New Zealand Portrait Gallery, Te Papa; walk around Parliament House and the Beehive.

New Zealand Portrait Gallery (P)

Address: Shed 11, Queen's Wharf, Customhouse Quay, Wellington Waterfront
Phone number: (04) 472 2298
Website: www.portraitgallery.nzl.org
Gallery Director: Avenal McKinnon
Building: Edwardian heritage building, formerly a wharf-side store.
Opening times: 10.30 am to 4.30 pm daily.
Admission charges: Free
Guided tours: On request
Wheelchair access: Yes
Toilets: Yes

The New Zealand Portrait Gallery is a significant visual archive of the many faces of New Zealand. From the celebrated to the seldom seen, poets to prime ministers, visionaries to villains, actors to activists, the New Zealand Portrait Gallery defines the unique qualities of Aotearoa New Zealand. The portraits speak of who we are, regardless of our origins, and provide visitors with powerful insights into our country, illuminating our past and even giving glimpses of our future.

Collection: The gallery is building and holding in trust for the nation a collection of portraits – painted, sculpted, electronically recorded – that reflect the history, developments and personalities of our country. Among the collection are portraits of Sir Edmund Hillary, Sir Peter Blake, James K. Baxter, Janet Frame, Michael Hill, Alan MacDiarmid, Barnaby Weir and the Rev. Henry Williams.

Exhibition schedule: Refer to the gallery website for current and future exhibitions.

Artists represented: Martin Ball, William Beetham, Harriet Bright, Helen Crane, Nick Cuthell, Frederick Ellis, Jacqueline Fahey, Irene Ferguson, John Fuller, Kevin Judd, Marianne Muggeridge, James Nairn, Mark Olsen, Evelyn Page, James Paton, Juliet Peter, Gaylene Preston, Glenda Randerson, Harry Linley Richardson, Beverley Shore Bennett, Garth Tapper, Murray Webb, Stephen Martyn Welch and Freeman White.
Where to eat: There are restaurants and bars adjacent to the gallery.
What else to do nearby: Follow the Writer's Walk along the waterfront to Te Papa.

Ngaio Fine Arts (D)

Address: 53B Ottawa Road, Ngaio
Phone number: (04) 479 0291
Website: www.ngaiofinearts.co.nz
Gallery Director: Suzanne Beer
Opening times: 10 am to 5 pm Monday to
Friday; 10 am to 4 pm Saturday.
Admission charges: Free
Guided tours: No
Wheelchair access: Yes, with assistance.
Toilets: No

Ngaio is located in one of Wellington's inner northern suburbs just 10 minutes' drive from the inner city. Ngaio Fine Arts is a high quality suburban gallery. It is small but select, showing a professional standard of art and specialising in early investment and collectable works. They are able to give advice on art and are happy if you are just browsing. There is free parking in front of the gallery and also in the large car park behind the shops.

Collection: Exhibits traditional and impressionist style works by leading New Zealand artists. The gallery specialises in early New Zealand and European investment work.
Exhibition schedule: Regular exhibitions April to November. Refer to the gallery website for current and future exhibitions.
Artists represented: Neil Bartlett, Brian Baxter, Peter Beadle, Michael Blow, Bill Burke, Colette Cheyne, Eugenea, Gaston De Vel, Ian Hamlin, Peter O'Hagan, Jacky Pearson, J. K. Reed, Colin Wynn. Early investment work as available by: Isobel Field, Frances Hodgkins, Peter McIntyre, James Nairn, D. K. Richmond, Cedric Savage, Margaret Stoddart, Sydney Lough Thompson, earlier colonial artists and other collectable artists.
Where to eat: There are a number of local cafés for brunch, lunch or coffee.
What else to do nearby: Go shopping; plan a bush walk.

Rona Gallery (D)

Address: 151 Muritai Road, Eastbourne
Phone number: (04) 562 8062
Website: www.art-gallery-newzealand.com
Gallery Director: Richard Ponder
Opening times: 10 am to 5 pm Monday to
Friday; 10 am to 4.30 pm Saturday;
11 am to 4.30 pm Sunday.
Admission charges: Free
Guided tours: By appointment
Wheelchair access: Yes
Toilets: No

Rona Gallery is a warm friendly space in the seaside community of Eastbourne. More than just a seaside gallery, Gallery Director Richard Ponder carefully selects his artists focusing on technique, attention to detail and composition. He is interested in both style and substance, because a painting should be treasured. Richard says, 'The mark of great art is that the more you see it, the more you like it.' From Mike Ponder's iconic representations of the rural heartland to Ken Hunt's realism and attention to detail, and Richard's bold, inspirational use of colour – Rona Gallery should not be missed on any tour of New Zealand.

Collection: Richard Ponder
Exhibition schedule: Refer to the gallery website for current and future exhibitions.
Artists represented: Richard Ponder, Michael Ponder, Ken Hunt, Darcy Nicholas, Wellesley Binding.
Where to eat: Try The Beach Café & Restaurant, Lemongrass Café, Lifeboat Tavern.
What else to do nearby: Enjoy bush walks and the beaches; shop in Eastbourne village; the swimming pool and park are all nearby.

Shona Moller Gallery (A)

Address: 42 Cable Street, Wellington (opposite Te Papa)
Phone number: (04) 939 9266
Website: www.shonamoller.com
Gallery Director: Bryce Moller
Building: Portal building

Opening times: 10.30 am to 4.30 pm Wednesday to Sunday.
Admission charges: Free
Guided tours: No
Wheelchair access: Yes
Toilets: Yes

Wellington artist Shona Moller has had her studio at Paraparaumu Beach since 1999 and her gallery in Wellington city since 2003. Recently returned from her sell-out solo exhibition in central London, Shona prefers to deal directly with the public. The resulting artistic freedom allows Shona to explore and display a variety of paintings and sculptures.

Collection: The gallery does not have a permanent collection.
Exhibition schedule: The gallery does not have an exhibition schedule.
Artist represented: Shona Moller
Where to eat: There are many eateries on the waterfront, Oriental Parade and Courtenay Place.
What else to do nearby: Visit Te Papa and City Gallery Wellington; view the Museum Hotel art collection.

Shona Moller Gallery

Solander Works on Paper (D)

Address: 218C Willis Street, Te Aro
Phone number: (04) 920 0913
Website: www.solandergallery.co.nz
Gallery Directors: Paulette Robinson and Vincent Drane
Opening times: 10 am to 5.30 pm Tuesday to Friday.
Admission charges: Free
Guided tours: Guided tours, floor talks and demonstrations by appointment.
Wheelchair access: Yes
Toilets: Yes

Solander Works on Paper is Wellington's specialist gallery for contemporary works on paper. Solander is in the midst of Wellington's vibrant art precinct. The gallery represents over 50 New Zealand and international artists with regular feature exhibitions and an extensive selection of works on permanent display. Works encompass contemporary drawings and watercolours and limited edition artist prints, including etchings, screen prints, woodcuts and mezzotints. Directors Paulette Robinson and Vincent Drane are enthusiastic about sharing their passion for works on paper with collectors, corporate buyers and those new to works on paper and printmaking.

Collection: The gallery does not have a permanent collection.
Exhibition schedule: Feature exhibitions are held every 5 weeks. Refer to the gallery website for current and future exhibitions.
Artists represented: Alex Milsom, Ben Reid, Catherine Macdonald, Chris Adams, Ellen Giggenbach, Faith McManus, Fleur Williams, Graham Hall, Inge Doesburg, Jacqueline Aust,

Jo Ogier, Kathryn Madill, Kim Lowe, Locust Jones, Lynn Taylor, Margaret Silverwood, Mark Graver, Martin Poppelwell, Marty Vreede, Michele Bryant, Michel Tuffery, Sam Broad, Simon Kaan, Stanley Palmer, Vanessa Edwards.

Where to eat: The gallery is located 200 metres from Cuba Street Mall where you will find a selection of cafés, restaurants and bars.

What else to do nearby: There are many galleries, independent designers and cafés nearby.

Suite Gallery (D)

Address: Level 2, 147 Cuba Street, Wellington
Phone number: (04) 976 7663
Website: www.suite.co.nz
Gallery Director: David Alsop
Building: Suite Gallery shares the building with Enjoy Public Art Gallery and Peter McLeavey Gallery.

Opening times: 11 am to 5 pm Wednesday to Friday; 11 am to 4 pm Saturday; after hours by appointment.
Admission charges: Free
Guided tours: By appointment
Wheelchair access: No
Toilets: Yes

Established in 2007, Suite Gallery recently moved from Newtown to the top of the Cuba Street gallery precinct. Suite Gallery represents a select group of prominent New Zealand artists. On occasions they present exhibitions by guest local and international artists. This gallery was the first private gallery in the southern hemisphere to exhibit works by celebrated Dutch photographer Desiree Dolron and Sweden-based, English-born artist James Aldridge. Suite also operates a project gallery out of a garage at 108 Oriental Parade, Wellington. Suite Gallery supports the publication of books and catalogues for its artists under the monograph Suite Publishing.

Collection: The gallery does not have a permanent collection.

Exhibition schedule: Refer to the gallery website for current and future exhibitions, and an archive of previous exhibitions.

Artists represented: Ans Westra, Irene Ferguson, Neil Pardington, Arie Hellendoorn, Fiona Pardington, Douglas Stichbury, Roger Boyce, Bruce Connew, Robert Cherry, Anton Parsons, Wayne Youle, Geoffrey Notman.

Where to eat: Scopa Caffe Cucina, Ernesto, Floriditas Café and Restaurant are all excellent choices.

What else to do nearby: Visit Enjoy Public Art Gallery and Peter McLeavey Gallery; stroll through the vibrant Cuba Mall.

Suite Gallery

The Dowse Art Museum (P)

Address: *45 Laings Road, Lower Hutt*
Phone number: *(04) 570 6500*
Website: *www.dowse.org.nz*
Gallery Director: *Cam McCracken*
Building: *Completely revamped in 2006 by Athfield Architects, the Dowse houses 11 exhibition spaces, several multi-purpose* *activity spaces, a courtyard and shop.*
Opening times: *10 am to 4.30 pm Monday to Friday; 10 am to 5 pm Saturday and Sunday.*
Admission charges: *Free*
Guided tours: *On request*
Wheelchair access: *Yes*
Toilets: *Yes*

The Dowse Art Museum is a contemporary art museum located in the satellite city of Lower Hutt just 15 minutes' drive from downtown Wellington. The Dowse has a proud reputation for presenting cutting-edge exhibitions by established and emerging artists alongside decorative arts and design. The family lounge offers hands-on activities for children and their caregivers. A busy events programme complements each exhibition season with the monthly Late Lounge (open late session with performances by bands and solo artists) being particularly popular.

Collection: The collection contains over 3000 works with a special focus on New Zealand decorative arts, jewellery, ceramics and textiles.
Exhibition schedule: A changing exhibition programme of contemporary art and design, including decorative arts, photography, furniture, sculpture and jewellery. Refer to the gallery website for current and future exhibitions.
Artists represented: Mainly contemporary New Zealand artists but international artists are showcased from time to time.
Where to eat: Café Reka is on-site.
What else to do nearby: Refer to www.huttcity.govt.nz/Leisure--Culture for local attractions, such as heritage trails, the Petone Settlers Museum, local galleries and parks.

The Dowse Art Museum

South Island

Marlborough/Nelson/Tasman

Bronte Art Gallery (A)

Address: 122 Bronte Road East, Nelson
Phone number: (03) 540 2579
Website: www.brontegallery.co.nz
Gallery Director: Darryl Robertson
Building: Purpose-built gallery and art studio
Opening times: 9 am to 5.30 pm daily
(summer); 9 am to 4.30 pm (winter).
Admission charges: Free
Guided tours: No
Wheelchair access: Yes, limited access is available with help from the gallery.
Toilets: No

Bronte Art Gallery was established in 1986 in a purpose-built gallery and art studio for well-known New Zealand artists Darryl Robertson and Lesley Jacka Robertson. It is a much loved and revisited gallery situated in a very relaxed environment next to the inspiring Waimea inlet on the stunning Bronte Peninsula. Paintings in acrylic and pencil on canvas and board are expressive and contemporary original works suitable for collector and tourist. Robertson's works are collected and held in museums, art galleries and private collections in New Zealand and around the world. Modern, original and iconic sculptural works combining clay, wood and metal are on display. Six quality holiday cottages overlook the inlet and olives, apples, grapes and a winemaker are all very close to Bronte Art Gallery.

Collection: Permanent collection of resident artists' work.
Exhibition schedule: The gallery holds ongoing exhibitions of Darryl Robertson's new works in sculpture and painting, as well as exhibitions of paintings by Lesley Jacka Robertson. This is the first place to view new work and meet the artists.
Artists represented: Darryl Robertson, Lesley Jacka Robertson
Where to eat: Try The Playhouse Performance Café & Theatre, Wharfside Restaurant and Bar,

Apple Shed Café and Bar, Golden Bear Brewery and The Naked Bun Patisserie & Café.
What else to do nearby: Visit a local vineyard – Rimu Grove Winery, Wollaston Estate Winery and Gallery or Seifried Winery; walk along Mapua Wharf for cafés and boutique shopping; take a trip to Rabbit Island beach and picnic area.

Cool Store Gallery (D)

Address: 7 Aranui Road, Mapua
Phone number: (03) 540 3778
Website: www.coolstoregallery.co.nz
Gallery Directors: Tricia Morrison and Emma Hope
Opening times: 10.30 am to 5.30 pm (summer); 11 am to 4.30 pm (winter).
Admission charges: Free
Guided tours: No
Wheelchair access: Yes
Toilets: Public toilets nearby

Established in 2001 the Cool Store Gallery is an experience for any art lover and not worth missing. It is located at the popular destination of Mapua Wharf, a scenic 25-minute drive from Nelson. The gallery showcases a lively and diverse range of quality works from over 150 artists, sculptors and jewellers. All works are proudly and exclusively created in New Zealand with the majority of them made locally.

Collection: The gallery does not have a permanent collection.
Exhibition schedule: Exhibitions are held at the rear of the gallery, sometimes at the request of artists or by the gallery.
Artists represented: Helen Back, Barbara Blewman, Sue Dasler, Dean Raybould, Sue Syme, Adam Styles, Lloyd Harwood, Andy Waugh, Llew Summers, Ross Richards, Mike Perry, Shane Hansen, Merve Sarson, Rinopai, Nic Wooding, Ashley Hilton, Deborah Walsh, Justin Ferguson, Michelle Domett.
Where to eat: The Apple Shed Café and Bar, Wharfside Restaurant and Bar, Hamish's Ice Cream Parlour & Café, Golden Bear Brewery and The Smokehouse Takeaway are all 2 minutes walk away.
What else to do nearby: Enjoy the scenic views; shop at Touch the Sea Aquarium & Gift Shop, Le Havre Collections (French-style interior design shop) and Forest Fusion Functional Art.

Copper Beech Gallery (A)

Address: 240 Thorp Street, Motueka
Phone number: (03) 528 7456
Website: www.copperbeechgallery.co.nz
Gallery Director: John Gatenby
Building: Private residence
Opening times: Open daily; if you are making a special trip, phone to avoid disappointment.
Admission charges: Free
Guided tours: No
Wheelchair access: Yes
Toilets: No

An internationally acclaimed artist, John Gatenby has painted for most of his life, pursuing his passion full-time for the last 20 years. John's gallery is situated in about 1 hectare of sculptured grounds of his home and is just 5 minutes from central Motueka. His finely honed style has gained him a global following and his faithful representations of the countryside and wildlife he loves are found in collections worldwide. John's landscapes – from the mountains to the sea – celebrate the ambience, grandeur and awe-inspiring nature of New Zealand's great outdoors. His New Zealand native bird paintings capture and represent the true essence of the bird and its uniqueness. John's work captures his strong affinity with nature, and his sensitivity for his subject is reflected in a meticulous attention to detail and his ability to capture its magnificence. He uses acrylics, which capture the rich landscape colours on archive quality board.

Collection: The gallery displays artwork by John Gatenby.
Exhibition schedule: The gallery does not hold exhibitions.
Artist represented: John Gatenby
Where to eat: Up The Garden Path Café is recommended.
What else to do nearby: Visit Abel Tasman National Park with its golden beaches for hiking, boating and kayaking; visit Kahurangi National Park and numerous nearby wineries and artisans.

EarthSea Gallery (A)

Address: 76 Boyle Street, Clifton, Takaka, Golden Bay
Phone number: (03) 525 7007
Website: www.earthseagallery.com
Gallery Director: Kerry Ann Geen
Opening times: 10 am to 5 pm (summer). Winter hours are variable but the gallery is open when Peter is working in his studio, or phone for an appointment.
Admission charges: Free
Guided tours: No
Wheelchair access: Yes
Toilets: No

EarthSea Gallery is the studio and gallery of renowned New Zealand landscape artist Peter Geen. It is located near Pohara Beach, Golden Bay, on the edge of the Motupipi Estuary en route to the golf course and historic Clifton Cemetery. The gallery displays only Peter's New Zealand landscape paintings in oil and acrylics and reproduction giclée prints on canvas and watercolour paper.

Collection: The gallery does not have a permanent collection.
Exhibition schedule: The gallery does not hold exhibitions.
Artist represented: Peter Geen
Where to eat: Try Penguin Café and Bar, Ratanui Lodge, The Wholemeal Café, The Mussel Inn and The Naked Possum Café.
What else to do nearby: Golden Bay is the gateway to world-class walking tracks – the Heaphy Track and Abel Tasman Coastal Track, the famous Farewell Spit and Te Waikoropupu

(Pupu) Springs. On the west coast, the adventurous traveller will discover wild coastal beaches, massive dunes, cliffs, arches and caves. Activities include kayaking, rock climbing, caving, windsurfing, fishing, whitebaiting and scalloping. Golden Bay has a vibrant art and craft community and a wide selection of cafés and restaurants.

Marilyn Andrews Gallery (A)

Address: 221 Brook Street, Nelson
Phone number: (03) 548 9400
Website: www.marilynandrewsart.co.nz
Gallery Director: Marilyn Andrews
Building: Private residence
Opening times: Open most days and by appointment. Please phone first.
Admission charges: Free
Guided tours: No
Wheelchair access: Yes but difficult
Toilets: Yes

This is an intimate home gallery showing the work of Nelson artist Marilyn Andrews who is primarily a landscape artist. The gallery is in an idyllic setting beside a stream in the beautiful Brook Valley, only a 5-minute drive from Nelson city centre. Marilyn is available to give you personal service in selecting a piece of art from her large range of landscapes: expressive, vibrant and colourful paintings and assemblage pieces. Marilyn, who has work in collections worldwide, also accepts commissions and will advise and collaborate with you to create exactly what you have in mind and express your special personal ideas. She can arrange packaging and freight locally, nationally and internationally. A range of Marilyn's greeting cards and unique calendars are also available.

Collection: The gallery displays artwork by Marilyn Andrews.
Exhibition schedule: The gallery does not hold regular exhibitions.
Artist represented: Marilyn Andrews
Where to eat: There are cafés and restaurants in nearby Nelson city centre.
What else to do nearby: Walk the old tramline track from the Brook Valley to the Dun Mountain; climb the Grampians and view Nelson city and Tasman Bay.

Meadowbank Gallery (A)

Address: 925 Waiwhero Road, Ngatimoti, RD1, Motueka
Phone number: (03) 526 8623
Website: www.annebannock.co.nz
Gallery Director: Anne Bannock
Building: Historic woolshed and converted milking shed
Opening times: 10 am to 5.30 pm daily (October to April), or by appointment. If making a special trip, please phone to avoid disappointment.
Admission charges: Free
Guided tours: No
Wheelchair access: Yes
Toilets: Yes

Meadowbank Gallery is situated in an historic woolshed on the artist's property at Ngatimoti, 20 minutes' drive from Motueka and 50 minutes from Nelson. It is located in the beautiful and tranquil Orinoco Valley and looks towards the mountains of the Kahurangi National Park. The Orinoco Stream meanders through the property on its way to the nearby Motueka River. Anne Bannock is the sole artist, having pursued her love of art with a freedom of spirit that has allowed her to experiment with a full spectrum of styles and media. Her subjects range from landscapes to still life and styles that are both bold and delicate. Many artworks can

Meadowbank Gallery

be found in collections around the world, including the United Kingdom, Europe, the United States of America, Australia, Canada and South Africa. Eight accepted entries from the World of Wearable Art show covering a number of years are also on display.

Collection: Art by Anne Bannock and World of Wearable Art accepted entries.
Exhibition schedule: Ongoing
Artist represented: Anne Bannock
Where to eat: There are two restaurants within a 10-minute drive and Motueka is just 20 minutes away.
What else to do nearby: The property has a challenging hedge maze. Motueka River is 5 minutes' drive away and is suitable for swimming, fishing and kayaking. A 35-minute drive will take you to Kahurangi National Park where there are both short and long walks.

Millennium Art Gallery (P)

Address: Cnr Seymour and Alfred Streets, Blenheim
Phone number: (03) 579 2001
Website: www.marlboroughart.org.nz
Gallery Director: Cressida Bishop
Opening times: 10.30 am to 4.30 pm Monday to Friday; 1 pm to 4 pm Saturday, Sunday and public holidays. Closed Christmas Day,

Boxing Day and New Year's Day.
Admission charges: Gold coin donation for adults, free for children.
Guided tours: Yes, contact the gallery for more information.
Wheelchair access: Yes
Toilets: Public toilets nearby

The Millennium Art Gallery opened in December 1999 and is Marlborough's public art gallery. It is located in the centre of Blenheim opposite Seymour Square and presents a high quality, varied programme of regularly changing art exhibitions and events. The gallery's exhibitions feature significant New Zealand artists, including Ralph Hotere, Bill Culbert

Millennium Art Gallery

and Frances Hodgkins, in both nationally touring and locally generated exhibitions. Emphasis is also placed on community-focused exhibitions that are developed in conjunction with other local events and organisations and include the work of Marlborough artists, iwi and school children. A not-for-profit organisation governed by a charitable trust and professionally managed, the gallery's operation is supported by an extensive network of volunteers. To generate funds to support the gallery's exhibition programme, art and picture books, cards, local art and jewellery are available to purchase in the gallery shop.

Collection: Nationally and internationally significant artists who have a connection with Marlborough are represented. The permanent collection includes works by Bill Culbert, Iosefa Leo, J. S. Parker, Don Peebles, Marilynn Webb and Sir Toss Woollaston. They also actively collect for the library collection, which contains fine art publications, magazines, exhibition catalogues and media clippings. Many of the donors of works to this collection have a history of supporting the Millennium Art Gallery. Several of the works are by artists who have exhibited at the gallery.

Exhibition schedule: Refer to the gallery or their website for current and future exhibitions.
Where to eat: There are eateries located nearby.
What else to do nearby: Take a walk in Seymour Square and Pollard Park; shop in the town centre.

MONZA (More Outstanding New Zealand Art) (D)

Address: *25 Commercial Street, Takaka, Golden Bay*
Phone number: *(03) 525 8510*
Website: *www.monza.co.nz*
Gallery Director: *Philly Hall*
Building: *Ground level of a charming old colonial wooden building (circa 1900)*

Opening times: *10 am to 5 pm daily (summer); winter hours are variable.*
Admission charges: *Free*
Guided tours: *No*
Wheelchair access: *Yes*
Toilets: *No*

Monza Gallery showcases exclusive local art by Golden Bay artists. Visitors are enchanted by the warm, welcoming atmosphere and the exceptional range and quality of art, from the small and quirky to large striking works. Paintings, ceramics, jewellery, sculpture and fibre art provide a visual feast!

Collection: Painters: Robin Slow, Dean Raybould, Geoffrey Heath, Robyn Fullerton, Kathy Reilly, araLyn Doiron, Kare Grayson, Philly Hall. Sculptors: Jocelynne Bacci, Lorraine Polglase. Jewellers: Nic Wooding, Chris Bone, Claire Prebble, Jean Burgers, Reg Harvey-Smith. Fibre artists: Sarah Hornibrooke, Maureen Harte, Bronwynn Billens.

Exhibition schedule: A mostly permanent display that constantly changes and evolves. The gallery occasionally holds solo or group exhibitions.
Artists represented: The gallery represents approximately 55 local Golden Bay artists.
Where to eat: There are cafés in Takaka.
What else to do nearby: Explore the shops in town; visit Te Waikorupupu (Pupu) Springs, just 10 minutes' drive away, and the multitude of beautiful beaches within 20 minutes' drive from town.

MONZA

RED Gallery of Contemporary Art (D)

Address: 1 Bridge Street, Nelson
Phone number: (03) 548 2170
Website: www.redartgallery.com
Gallery Directors: Caroline Marshall and Sarah Sharp
Building: The Cock & Co. building is a former foundry and granary. Joseph Henry Cock was a prominent businessman in Nelson. In 1901 he formed Anchor Shipping and Foundry Limited, which played an important part in the economy of the Nelson region. Cock was described as kind, generous and sociable and was involved in the Bishop Suter Art Gallery (named after Bishop Suter, the second Bishop of Nelson) on whose board he served as a trustee.

Opening times: 8 am to 4 pm Monday to Friday; 9 am to 2 pm Saturday.
Admission charges: Free
Guided tours: No
Wheelchair access: No
Toilets: Yes

RED Gallery and The Morning Room Café are located in the main shopping area of Nelson. Artworks hang in a beautiful environment alongside furniture and oriental rugs. The gallery is in one of Nelson's oldest buildings, originally a foundry and granary, with wonderful matai floors and high ceilings. Ceramics, glass, jewellery, greeting cards and other interesting bits and pieces make this gallery a fascinating destination for locals and visitors alike. It also has a picture-framing studio.

Collection: The gallery does not have a permanent collection.
Exhibition schedule: The gallery has monthly openings.
Artists represented: Sally Papps, Brent Forbes, Sally Burton, Richard Adams, Barry Clarke, Austin Davies, Fane Flaws, John Robinson, Christine Boswijk, Ross Mitchell-Anyon, Kay van Dyke, Helen Riddell, Margaret Major, Genevieve Packer, Zoe Buchanan, Lloyd Harwood, Janet Bathgate, Nic Foster, and more.
Where to eat: Get great coffee at The Morning Room Café at RED Gallery or The Suter Gallery Café.
What else to do nearby: Walk in Anzac Park across the road and visit The Suter Art Gallery nearby on Bridge Street.

The Diversion Gallery (D)

Address: *Grove Mill Winery, 13 Waihopai Valley Road, Renwick, Blenheim*
Phone number: *(03) 572 8200 or 027 440 8121*
Website: *www.thediversion.co.nz*
Gallery Director: *Barbara Speedy*
Building: *Grove Mill Winery Cellar Door*
Opening times: *11 am to 5 pm daily; winter hours (May to September); after hours by appointment. Closed Good Friday, Anzac Day, Christmas Day, and New Year's Day.*
Admission charges: *Free*
Guided tours: *By appointment*
Wheelchair access: *Yes*
Toilets: *Yes*

Situated in the unique setting of the tasting room at Grove Mill Winery, The Diversion Gallery is a contemporary fine art gallery exhibiting senior collectible New Zealand artists and selected mid-career artists. It is about 15 minutes' drive from Blenheim and 35 minutes from Picton. The gallery is principal agent for Don Binney in New Zealand, with some earlier works in stock. The gallery's exhibitions include paintings, prints and sculpture, primarily new and recent works, and occasionally outdoor sculpture in the vineyard. Stock not on exhibition can be viewed by prior appointment with the director (stockroom off site). The gallery also represents Marlborough's nationally recognised abstract painter J. S. Parker. A visit to the studio of J. S. Parker can be organised by prior arrangement.

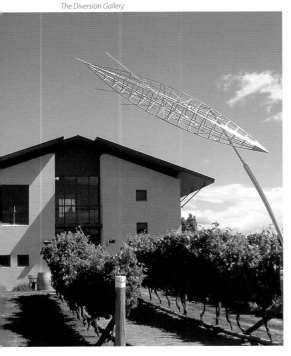
The Diversion Gallery

Collection: The gallery does not have a permanent collection.

Exhibition schedule: Exhibitions change every 6 to 8 weeks, openings Monday or Tuesday at 6 pm.

Artists represented: Don Binney, Graham Bennett, Barry Cleavin, Bing Dawe, Melvin Day, John Drawbridge, Don Driver, Fatu Feu'u, Kathryn Madill, J. S. Parker, Wayne Seyb, Michael Smither, Eion Stevens, Richard Adams, Llew Summers, Grahame Sydney, Jeff Thomson, Philip Trusttum, Marilynn Webb.

Where to eat: Enjoy the picnic area in the wetland – cheeseboards are available. There are restaurants at other wineries nearby.

What else to do nearby: Visit the vine library at Grove Mill (tasting in autumn); the award-winning wetland area; play pétanque. Enjoy lunch at other wineries nearby; visit the Omaka Aviation Heritage Centre, about 8 kilometres away.

West Coast

Brent Trolle Gallery (A)

Address: 13 Whitcombe Terrace, Hokitika
Phone number: (03) 755 7250
Website: www.brenttrolle.com
Gallery Director: Grace Trolle
Building: Private residence

Opening times: 9 am to late, open 7 days.
Admission charges: Free
Guided tours: No
Wheelchair access: Yes
Toilets: Yes, in artist's residence.

Set in the award-winning home garden of prominent New Zealand artist Brent Trolle this gallery is easily located by following the 'Art Gallery' signage off Tudor Street which is to the north of Hokitika township. The gallery displays works by Brent Trolle, a plein-air painter, and his son Lance Trolle, and has been established for over 35 years. It is the main outlet in New Zealand for both Brent and Lance's work and is open daily for visitors to enjoy.

Collection: Brent Trolle, Lance Trolle
Exhibition schedule: The gallery does not hold exhibitions.
Artists represented: This is a private gallery which features father and son works by Brent and Lance Trolle.
Where to eat: Hokitika cafés and restaurants are just 1 kilometre away.
What else to do nearby: Hokitika is the pounamu (greenstone or jade) capital of New Zealand; visit the local beach, Hokitika Gorge and Lake Kaniere Scenic Reserve.

Hale Gallery (A)

Address: 29A Broadway, Reefton
Phone number: 027 288 7498
Website: http://alisonhaleartist.vc.net.nz
Gallery Director: Alison Hale
Building: Historic wooden building
(circa 1900s)
Opening times: 9 am to 4 pm (summer); 10 am

to 4 pm (winter); after hours by appointment.
Admission charges: Free
Guided tours: By appointment, please
phone Alison Hale.
Wheelchair access: Yes
Toilets: Public toilets nearby on the main
street of Reefton.

The Hale Gallery is surrounded by the Victoria Forest Park in a picturesque historic gold mining town on the West Coast. Established by three local artists 12 years ago, it is an artist-run space and features established artists with a strong connection to the region. It exhibits both traditional and contemporary landscape and figurative work in oils and acrylics. The gallery has earned a strong reputation for its unique equine works in both contemporary and traditional oils on canvas and oil on glass.

Adjoining the gallery is another exhibition space, The Storekeeper, featuring emerging local artists, with a large working studio that is open to the public and provides interaction with some of the artists. Here watercolour, acrylic, oils and printmaking mediums are used. A smaller space connecting the two is the Smallbone Gallery for more intimate artworks, such as painting on ceramic tiles and local pottery. Only original artwork is exhibited in these spaces.

Collection: Alison Hale collection – *Brunner Mine Widows* (2009), *Start of Summer* (2010), *Pike River Unfolding* (2010).
Exhibition schedule: Constantly updated with new works.
Artists represented: Susan Ferguson, Alison Hale, Ruth Vaega, Anna Hollings, Chris H. Lewis, Michelle Green, Keith Wills.
Where to eat: The Future Dough Company Tearooms and Bakery is next door, and there are other eating establishments close by.
What else to do nearby: Visit Alison Hale's studio in the old Reefton Courthouse (Bridge Street), Black's Point Museum, Black's Point Pottery (by arrangement); enjoy Gold Mine Tours and The Bearded Miners' replica mining hut; visit The School of Mines; take historic town walks and varied bush walks; go trout fishing; children will love the amazing skate park and heated swimming pool.

Hokitika Craft Gallery (D)

Address: 25 Tancred Street, Hokitika	(summer); 8.30 am to 5 pm (winter).
Phone number: (03) 755 8802	**Admission charges:** Free
Website: www.hokitikacraftgallery.co.nz	**Guided tours:** On request
Gallery Director: There is no appointed director.	**Wheelchair access:** Yes
Opening times: 8.30 am to 8.30 pm daily	**Toilets:** No

A cooperative gallery featuring local painters and craftspeople in fibre, wood, pounamu (greenstone or jade), bone, silk, jewellery and pottery.

Collection: The gallery does not have a permanent collection.
Exhibition schedule: The gallery does not hold exhibitions.
Artists represented: Chris Weaver, Marc Zuckerman, Susan Brown, Fiona Carruthers, Peter Bishop, Jayme Anderson, Helen Oliver, Irene Richards, Andrew Nolan, Sarah Jolly, Jim Gordon, Roger Chapman, Andrew Austin, Alison Tibbles, Janice Harnett.
Where to eat: Stumpers Bar & Café, Village Bakers, Café de Paris are all recommended.
What else to do nearby: Browse the wide variety of shops; visit Lake Kaniere Scenic Reserve and Hokitika Gorge.

Hale Gallery

John Burns Gallery of Modern Art (A)

Address: *26C Weld Street, Hokitika*
Phone number: *(03) 755 7237*
Website: *www.johnburnsartist.co.nz*
Gallery Director: *John Burns*
Building: *Former warehouse*

Opening times: *9 am to 4.30 pm daily.*
Admission charges: *Free*
Guided tours: *On request*
Wheelchair access: *No*
Toilets: *No*

This is a private gallery featuring works of well-represented contemporary South Island artist John Burns. John Burns is a talented artist who has experimented with many mediums over his 30-year career. Using only what he considers to be the very best quality materials, John goes as far as using several different brands of paints to achieve different colours. He generally uses a palette of only eight colours, preferring to create colour himself. John is a modern artist always searching for something different and describes himself as being 'only a transporter'. John Burns Gallery is situated on the main street of Hokitika where all visitors are welcome.

Collection: In-house viewings of the following pieces: *Vikings of the Paradaxe*, *Bean*, *Dickheads*, *Otira* series, *Ladies*. These works can also be viewed on the gallery website.
Exhibition schedule: The exhibition schedule is ongoing. Refer to the gallery website for current and future exhibitions.
Artist represented: John Burns
Where to eat: Hokitika has a good selection of places to eat.
What else to do nearby: Hokitika is the pounamu (greenstone or jade) capital of New Zealand; catch the annual West Coast Whitebait Festival (September–October); enjoy magnificent scenery, the quietness of the area and the sandflies!

Canterbury

In February 2011, a major earthquake was experienced in Christchurch and many, many buildings in the city suffered catastrophic damage resulting in a very large number of businesses not reopening or closing for an uncertain amount of time. Some art galleries have been able to open their doors and welcome visitors once again, while other galleries have had to find new premises.

Aigantighe Art Museum (P)

Address: 49 Wai-iti Road, Timaru
Phone number: (03) 688 4424
Website: www.timaru.govt.nz/art-gallery
Gallery Director: Dr Fiona Ciaran
Building: The 1908 mansion that forms half of the building was the retirement home of Alexander and Helen Grant from Scotland who made their fortune sheep farming in New Zealand. Their art collection formed the beginning of Aigantighe's permanent collection. The modern wing was added in 1978.
Opening times: 10 am to 4 pm Tuesday to Friday; 12 pm to 4 pm Saturday and Sunday.
Admission charges: Free
Guided tours: By appointment
Wheelchair access: Yes
Toilets: Yes

The Aigantighe Art Museum (Aigantighe is Scottish Gaelic for 'at home' and is pronounced 'egg and tie') is renowned internationally for its collection and its innovative exhibition and education programmes. It was founded in 1956 by a Scottish family and now has the South Island's third largest public art museum collection. Aigantighe holds New Zealand, Pacific, Asian and European artworks from the 16th century to the present day. Its British Victorian painting collection is of great significance. In the modern wing, regional, national and international exhibitions are shown. The Aigantighe is well known for its extensive and innovative use and unique interpretation of its collection in entertaining, well-researched exhibitions. Aigantighe supports life-long learning and energetically launched a number of New Zealand art museum 'firsts', such as an 'Art Car', living sculptures and replica dress ups of historic paintings. During school holidays new programmes are themed around the exhibitions on show. The sculpture garden with work by African, Japanese and New Zealand sculptors is always open.

Collection: New Zealand, Pacific, Asian and European artworks from the 16th century to the present day, and an important British Victorian painting collection. Masterpieces by Charles

Aigantighe Art Museum

F. Goldie, Frances Hodgkins and Colin McCahon (born in Timaru) feature in a room dedicated especially to them and six new thematic exhibitions from the permanent collection are held in the House Gallery each year.

Exhibition schedule: Twenty-three regional, national, international and permanent collection exhibitions each year. Refer to the gallery website for current and future exhibitions.

Artists represented: This gallery does not represent individual artists.

Where to eat: See the many local cafés and restaurants.

What else to do nearby: Wander through the Aigantighe Art Gallery Sculpture Garden; visit Te Ana Rock Art Centre.

Alexis Fine Art Gallery (D)

Address: 359 Colombo Street, Sydenham Central Mall, Christchurch
Phone number: (03) 365 5800
Website: www.alexisinternational.co.nz
Gallery Director: Alexis Brown
Opening times: 10 am to 5 pm Monday to
Saturday; 11 am to 4 pm Sunday.
Admission charges: Free
Guided tours: On request
Wheelchair access: Yes
Toilets: Yes

Established in 2001, Alexis Fine Art Gallery is located in the Sydenham Central Mall in Christchurch. The gallery offers an impressive selection of original paintings and sculpture by both emerging and established New Zealand artists.

Collection: All the artists represented feature in the collection.

Exhibition schedule: Refer to the gallery website for current and future exhibitions.

Artists represented: Kees Bruin, Nathanael Provis, John Burns, Robin Slow, John Maillard,

Alexis Fine Art Gallery

David Lloyd, Paul James O'Hagan, Asheley Elizabeth, Doug Neil, Elana Daem, Carmen Simmonds, Sue James, Maxine Williams, Bill Thrupp, Kerry Fenton-Johns, Michael Hewson.
Where to eat: Underground Coffee Company is recommended.
What else to do nearby: The Sydenham Central Mall food court and shops are nearby.

Bryce Gallery (D)

Address: *122 Riccarton Road, Riccarton, Christchurch*
Phone number: *(03) 348 0064, 021 258 2691*
Website: *www.brycegallery.co.nz*
Gallery Director: *Denise Bryce*
Opening times: *10 am to 4 pm Monday to Friday; 10 am to 4 pm Saturday;*
11 am to 4 pm Sunday; after hours by appointment.
Admission charges: *Free*
Guided tours: *By appointment*
Wheelchair access: *Yes*
Toilets: *Yes*

Bryce Gallery is owned and operated by Denise Bryce and Bruce Church and was established in 2005. The gallery specialises in fine contemporary artworks from local artists, as well as from other New Zealand centres and also imports unique works from overseas – notably from Australia, the United States of America and Europe. The gallery displays a wonderful array of paintings, sculpture, limited edition giclées, prints and glass. Customer car parking is available at the rear of the building with access via Rimu or Kauri Streets. The gallery offers an in-home or office art consultancy service by appointment.

Collection: The gallery does not have a permanent collection.
Exhibition schedule: Refer to the gallery website for current and future exhibitions.
Artists represented: Mark Olsen, Julia Drake, Hamish Allan, Brian Dahlberg, Brian Baxter,

Brian Strong, Brian McCracken, Kirk Munro, Jan Rasmussen, Don McAra, Blair Greig, Alison Coulthurst, Dalene Meiring, Craig Fletcher, Lisa Wisse, Geoff Williams, Galina Kim, Mehrdad Tahan, Harold Coop, Kendall Perkins, Linda Vario, Nick Fedaeff, Philip Beadle, Kelvin McMillan, Richard Bolton and others.

Where to eat: Try Browsers Garden Café in the adjacent block or Columbus Coffee in Westfield Mall.

What else to do nearby: Westfield Mall is directly opposite for shopping; the heritage site Riccarton House and Bush with the colonial Deans Cottage is a short walk away.

Centre of Contemporary Art (CoCA) (P)

Address: *66 Gloucester Street, Christchurch*
Phone number: *(03) 366 7261*
Website: *www.coca.org.nz*
Gallery Director: *Warren Feeney*
Building: *CoCA's gallery is a purpose-built art gallery designed by architects Minson, Henning-Hanson and Dines and features 1000 square metres of exhibition space divided into six separate galleries.*

Opening times: *Phone or refer to www.coca.org.nz for confirmation of opening times.*
Admission charges: *Donation*
Guided tours: *Yes*
Wheelchair access: *Please phone gallery to confirm.*
Toilets: *Yes*

For more than 120 years the Centre of Contemporary Art (CoCA) has acted as one of New Zealand's most significant arts institutions. The gallery represents established and emerging artists, encompassing painting, printmaking, installation, design, craft and photography, with a commitment to quality and excellence. It provides exhibitions and work for sale from a wide variety of New Zealand artists, and has a special interest in Canterbury artists, featuring work from local painters every month. An open gallery sells work by contemporary Canterbury painters. CoCA also has one of the country's largest exhibiting galleries. An additional gallery space, the Selling Gallery, features a rotating exhibition of original art, established and historical works. The Centre provides a professional environment to view artists' work in an atmosphere that is open and welcoming. If you want to talk to the experts, CoCA offers education programmes, tours, valuations, an information service and advice for members, artists and the general public on the visual arts. CoCA aims to act as a centre for the dissemination of information and debate about contemporary art.

Collection: The comprehensive permanent collection features 19th- and 20th-century New Zealand artists.

Exhibition schedule: Refer to the gallery website for current and future exhibitions.

Artists represented: Doris Lusk, Dick Frizzell, Philip Trusttum, Sam Foley, Olivia Spencer-Bower and many more. Refer to the gallery website for a list of artists.

Where to eat: There is a selection of cafés and restaurants in the locality.

What else to do nearby: Punt on the beautiful Avon River; visit the Christchurch Botanical Gardens.

McAtamney Gallery

McAtamney Gallery (D)

Address: Old Post Office Building,
47–49 Talbot Street, Geraldine
Phone number: (03) 693 7292
Website: www.mcatamneygallery.co.nz
Gallery Directors: Carolyn McAtamney-Rasch
and Andrew Rasch
Building: A New Zealand Historic Places Trust
Category II listed building, the Old Post Office
Building is a handsome brick structure built
in 1908. The Timaru Post Office closed its
doors in April 1997. The building was sold at
auction to a private buyer in 2005.
Opening times: 10 am to 4.30 pm Monday to
Sunday, or by appointment.
Admission charges: Free
Guided tours: On request
Wheelchair access: No
Toilets: Yes

McAtamney Gallery opened 22 January 2011 occupying the upstairs space of the Old Post
Office Building on Talbot Street, Geraldine. Gallery directors Carolyn McAtamney-Rasch and
Andrew Rasch are representing a select group of established and emerging artists from
New Zealand and abroad with a strong focus on portraiture. Their interest is fundamentally
in modern and contemporary art practice featuring oil paintings, works on paper,
photography, printmaking and sculpture. Individual exhibiting spaces entitled 'Mail Room',
'The Box', 'Verde' and 'The Manse' combine with the character of the 1908 post office.
The gallery promotes a richness and diversity that will appeal to all art connoisseurs. The
distinctive nature of the individual works epitomises the extreme and creative values of the
artists and directors of the gallery.

Collection: John Badcock – *The Last Supper*, *Sermon* series, *Passing People*, *Lecture* series, *Stations of the Cross*. Susan Badcock – *Zero* (published by Di Halstead and Cathy Tuato'o Ross, 2006).
Exhibition schedule: Refer to the gallery website for current and future exhibitions.
Artists represented: John Badcock, Susan Badcock, Helen Badcock, Susan Wilson, James Robinson.
Where to eat: Verde Café Deli is behind the gallery.
What else to do nearby: Visit Geraldine Historical Society Museum; take a walk in Talbot Forest Scenic Reserve or Peel Forest; see Woodbury Memorial Library and Cemetery, and historic churches, such as the Church of St Anne's, Pleasant Valley.

Merivale Fine Arts (D)

Address: 194 Papanui Road, Merivale, Christchurch
Phone number: (03) 356 2538
Website: www.merivalefinearts.co.nz
Gallery Director: Don Goulter
Building: Gallery consists of 120 square metres of display space.

Opening times: 9 am to 5 pm Monday to Saturday; 11 am to 2 pm Sunday.
Admission charges: Free
Guided tours: No
Wheelchair access: Yes
Toilets: Public toilets nearby

This is Christchurch's designation gallery for discerning buyers of investment and historical New Zealand art. The gallery features over 400 works by contemporary and historical investment artists at any one time. Merivale Fine Arts are members of the United Kingdom Fine Art Trade Guild by invitation. It is a small family gallery owned by Don Goulter located in Christchurch's Merivale village-style mall, surrounded by antique shops, cafés, bars, designer brand fashion and jewellery stores. The gallery offers an international shipping service to all purchasers.

Collection: Don Binney, Charles F. Goldie, Graham Sydney, Rudi Gopas, J. Gully, John Gibb, Petrus van der Velden, Trevor Moffitt, Tom Esplin, Clark Esplin, Austen Deans, Ben Woollcombe, Douglas Badcock, Peter Beadle, Olivia Spencer-Bower, W. F. Moore, L.W.Wilson.
Exhibition schedule: Exhibitions are held quarterly through the year.
Artists represented: Many artists are represented by Merivale Fine Arts. Refer to the gallery website for a complete list.
Where to eat: There are numerous cafés, bars, restaurants and takeaway businesses in the shopping area at Merivale village.
What else to do nearby: Visit local shops and eateries.

Saffron Gallery of Art (D)

Address: *Main South Road,*
300 Hilton Highway, Washdyke
Phone number: *(03) 688 2994*
Website: *www.saffrongallery.co.nz*
Gallery Director: *Rosemary Walden*
Building: *Ken Wills Complex*
Opening times: *10 am to 5 pm Tuesday to*
Friday; 11 am to 4 pm Saturday;
closed Sunday and Monday.
Admission charges: *Free*
Guided tours: *No*
Wheelchair access: *Yes*
Toilets: *Yes*

The Saffron Gallery is situated at 300 Hilton Highway, Ken Wills Complex, on the main highway just north of Timaru. The focus of the gallery is to provide works of a collectible nature to the viewing public. Director Rosemary Walden is committed to promoting traditional and contemporary New Zealand art and can advise on all matters relating to the collection of art, both private and corporate. Saffron Gallery exhibits painting, sculpture and limited edition works on paper sourced from the studios of some of New Zealand's most significant artists. They also offer a variety of outstanding works from the secondary market. Saffron Gallery is dedicated to working with an exciting group of young and critically acclaimed award-winning New Zealand artists. It has a rigorous selection process, which is designed to ensure that clients are offered the best artwork from the emerging and rising stars of the New Zealand art world. On display you will find quality realistic, abstract, traditional and contemporary New Zealand art.

Collection: Refer to the gallery website for information on the collection.
Exhibition schedule: Refer to the gallery website for current and future exhibitions.
Artists represented: A. A. Deans, John Badcock, Richard Bolton, Douglas Badcock, W. F. Moore, Ben Woollcombe, Marilynn Webb, Colin Wynn, Ewan McDougall, Barry Cleavin, Clark Esplin, Neil Driver, Rosemary Campbell, John Emery, John Burns, Trevor Askin, Rachel Ratten, Jo Ogier, Roselyn Cloake, Bronwyn Shimmin, Philip Beadle, Peter Beadle, Rosy Thomas, Rachel Harre and Frank Malone, Michael Armstrong, Claire Beynon.
Where to eat: There is a coffee shop in the complex.
What else to do nearby: The complex includes a hairdresser, beauty clinic, furniture shop, house design, kitchen design, coffee shop and giftware shop.

Salamander Gallery (D)

Address: *17 Marriner Street, Sumner,*
Christchurch
Phone number: *(03) 365 9279*
Website: *www.salamandergallery.co.nz*
Gallery Director: *Anne Munro*
Building: *The Old Tram Station*
Opening times: *10 am to 5 pm Wednesday*
to Sunday, or by appointment.
Admission charges: *Free*
Guided tours: *No*
Wheelchair access: *No*
Toilets: *Yes*

Prior to the earthquake experienced in Christchurch in February 2011, Salamander Gallery operated from the Christchurch Arts Centre in Hereford Street. Due to extensive damage to the building, the gallery has been relocated to Sumner and now welcomes visitors. The gallery represents both established and emerging New Zealand artists working in printmaking, painting and sculpture.

Collection: The gallery does not have a permanent collection.

Exhibition schedule: Refer to the gallery website for current and future exhibitions.

Artists represented: Trevor Askin, Andrew Bond, Dean Buchanan, Katy Buess, Andrew Craig, Sue Cooke, Inge Doesburg, Dagmar Dyck, Brent Forbes, Barbara Graham, Bob Kerr, Yong-Hyun Kwon, Jay Linden, Catherine Macdonald, Jo Ogier, Jenna Packer, Stanley Palmer, Kathy Reilly, Annie Smits Sandano, Michel Tuffery, Sheyne Tuffery, Frith Wilkinson, Tracey Williams, Fatu Feu'u.

Where to eat: Jo's Garage is next door and there are other cafés close by.

What else to do nearby: The gallery is one block away from the beach. There are great cafés, a movie theatre, unique shops and walking access to the surrounding hills.

Otago

Alan Waters Art Gallery (A)

Address: *81 Pigeon Rock Road (off Cornish Point Road), Bannockburn, RD2, Cromwell*
Phone number: *(03) 445 4723 or 021 076 8993*
Website: *www.alanwatersart.co.nz*
Gallery Director: *Alan Waters*
Building: *Adjacent to the artist's residence*

Opening times: *1 pm to 5 pm daily, or please phone for an appointment.*
Admission charges: *Free*
Guided tours: *No*
Wheelchair access: *Yes*
Toilets: *Yes*

Alan Waters has been a full-time artist for 17 years. His contemporary gallery and studio is probably the highest private art gallery in New Zealand. It is perched on a rocky escarpment in the historic rugged hinterland of the Cairnmuir Ranges at Bannockburn and overlooks the extensive Cromwell Valley and Lake Dunstan. Although Alan sometimes uses acrylic, his paintings are widely recognised for his mastery of that beautiful but elusive medium, watercolour. Certainly not one to follow any trends, he paints his own way every time. His work can be described as unique, whimsical, abstract, beautiful, extraordinary, disbelieving and unexpected. This well-known artist's gallery now receives visitors from all around the world, and his work is held in private collections worldwide. The views alone are well worth the trip up the hill.

Collection: Alan Waters
Exhibition schedule: Contact the gallery for exhibition information.
Artist represented: Alan Waters
Where to eat: There are various local cafés and restaurants in Cromwell town.
What else to do nearby: Visit Cromwell Museum; take a Bannock Historic Goldfields Tour; choose some of the numerous wineries to visit; get into hiking, cycling, skiing, adventure sports and other activities.

Arrowtown Gallery (D)

Address: *2/40–44 Buckingham Street, Arrowtown*
Phone number: *(03) 442 1755*
Website: *www.arrowtowngallery.co.nz*
Gallery Director: *Simon Beadle*

Opening times: *10 am to 4.30 pm daily.*
Admission charges: *Free*
Guided tours: *No*
Wheelchair access: *Yes*
Toilets: *Public toilets nearby*

The Arrowtown Gallery is located in the main street of the historic village of Arrowtown. The gallery has a diverse range of work from local artists including Peter Beadle, a talented and respected landscape artist who works in oils, and Russ McLean who presents stunning landscape photography. Also on display is work by other artists from New Zealand and Australia, such as Philippa Bentley, Paul Hanrahan, Steve Harris and Kelvin Mann. These artists work in a range of unique styles and mediums, including oil, watercolour, acrylic and photography, providing the visitor with a varied selection to linger over. Philippa Bentley's pieces feature screen-printed and hand-coloured insects on upcycled weatherboards or paper. Watercolours by Paul Hanrahan, whose work is noted for its impressionistic narratives of people going about their everyday lives, is always interesting and pleasing on the eye. An experienced framer is able to provide specialist advice and there is a range of art books, cards and handmade photograph frames available for purchase.

Collection: The gallery does not have a permanent collection.
Exhibition schedule: Exhibitions vary. Refer to the gallery website for current and future exhibitions.
Artists represented: Peter Beadle, Philippa Bentley, Robin Brisker, Antonia Haege, Paul Hanrahan, Steve Harris, Russ McLean, Kelvin Mann, Marion Vialade.
Where to eat: There is a café next door to the gallery, and Arrowtown has a good selection of places to eat.
What else to do nearby: The Lakes District Museum houses the local i-SITE, which provides information for a wide range of activities in and around the area.

Arrowtown was established in 1862. It was the discovery of gold in the Arrow River which led miners by their thousand into the district and resulted in the formation of settlements adjacent to the gold diggings. After the hype of the gold rush diminished in the early 1900s, Arrowtown has continued to thrive as a small satellite town to Queenstown and as a base for agriculture in this part of the basin. In recent years Arrowtown has become increasingly recognised as a living historic town, attracting many visitors from wider New Zealand and all over the world. Strict preservation orders protect the originality of the town's historic buildings, and the excellent Lakes District Museum, which is very close to the gallery, has many displays pertaining to the pioneering past of the district. It has become recognised as the walking and biking centre of Wakatipu and many walking trails and cycle tracks of the area either start or finish in the town.

Artbay Gallery (D)

Address: Level 1, The Mountaineer Building, 32 Rees Street, Queenstown
Phone number: (03) 442 9090 or 021 499 477
Website: www.artbay.co.nz
Gallery Director: Pauline Bianchi
Building: The Mountaineer Building has been known as 'The Mountaineer' since 1885. Originally The Prince of Wales Hotel, the building was partly demolished and rebuilt in stone and concrete in 1885. The architect Frederick W. Burwell designed the façade in 1884 for the renovation.
Opening times: 11 am to 5.30 pm Monday to Saturday; 12 pm to 4 pm Sunday.
Admission charges: Free
Guided tours: On request
Wheelchair access: Yes
Toilets: Yes

From the striking industrial-styled space in the Mountaineer Building, Artbay operates not only as a gallery, but also as an art destination. Every piece of artwork and sculpture is hand chosen from their stable of 60 artists. The gallery specialises in offering two collections – New Zealand contemporary art (modern abstracts and detailed works with iconic themes), and New Zealand uber art (exploratory and challenging pieces often in mixed media). Artbay Gallery provides a personalised art consultancy service and has assisted in creating art collections, advising on art for luxury lodges, homes, hotels and commercial spaces. Their service includes provision of art concepts, commissioning artwork, right through to framing and installation.

Artbay Gallery

Collection: The gallery does not have a permanent art collection.
Exhibition schedule: Exhibitions held bimonthly. Refer to the gallery website for current and future exhibitions.
Artists represented: Virginia Leonard, Hope Gibbons, Alan Waters, Simon Morrison-Deaker, Mandy Emerson, Jo Ogier, John Shewry, Kathryn Furniss, Fiona Gedson, Shane Hansen, Rachel Hirabayashi, Craig Primrose, Rachael Errington, Rae West, Tony Cribb, Jeri Elliot, Jane Kellahan, John Burns, Elizabeth Morrison-Dulieu and sculptors Pedro Bianchi, Mark Hill, Dan Kelly, Sean Crawford, Shane Woolridge.
Where to eat: There is a café next door to the gallery.
What else to do nearby: The area has cafés, a spa, upmarket clothing stores, lakefront walk, restaurants and bars, and numerous sightseeing options.

Central Art Gallery (D)

Address: *71 Beach Street, Queenstown*
Phone number: *(03) 442 7025*
Website: *www.centralart.co.nz*
Gallery Director: *Julia Milley*
Opening times: *10 am to 10 pm Monday to Friday; 11 am to 10 pm Saturday and Sunday.*

Admission charges: *Free*
Guided tours: *Knowledgeable staff are always available to discuss the artists and their background with clients.*
Wheelchair access: *Yes*
Toilets: *Yes*

Central Art Gallery in Queenstown is one of New Zealand's oldest privately owned galleries of fine art and displays works from many renowned artists. There is a wide selection of contemporary art or traditional paintings by New Zealand and international artists for the visitor to enjoy. From time to time, reputable artists will create a new painting in the gallery, allowing visitors to view the artist at work.

Collection: The gallery does not have a permanent collection.
Exhibition schedule: Ongoing exhibition schedule. Refer to the gallery website for current and future exhibitions.
Artists represented: Richard Wilson, Tim Wilson, Ralph Hotere, Lisa Wisse, Peter Beadle, Brian McCracken, Kelvin McMillan, Nigel Wilson, Mark Rodgers, Graham Brinsley, Johnny Groome, Clark Esplin, Malcolm Mason, Thomas Brown, Mark Zhu, Philip Beadle, J. K. Reed, Melanie Gurnsey-Hammett, Simon Williams.
Where to eat: Try the 19th Restaurant or Pub On Wharf across the road.
What else to do nearby: Visit the Kiwi Birdlife Park or Underwater World Aquarium; ride the Skyline Gondolas; take a lake cruise; or for the more adventurous try Off Road Adventures.

Dunedin Public Art Gallery (P)

Address: *30 The Octagon, Dunedin*
Phone number: *(03) 474 3240*
Website: *www.dunedin.art.museum*
Gallery Director: *Elizabeth Caldwell*
Opening times: *10 am to 5 pm daily. Closed Christmas Day.*

Admission charges: *Free*
Guided tours: *By appointment*
Wheelchair access: *Yes*
Toilets: *Yes, with a dedicated area for mothers and babies.*

The Dunedin Public Art Gallery is one of New Zealand's four major metropolitan art galleries. Established during Dunedin's gold-rush boom in 1884, the gallery was New Zealand's first public art gallery and is renowned today for the richness of its collection, its close working relationship with major New Zealand artists, its visiting artist programme and the quality of its exhibition and publishing programmes. It continues to flourish as one of New Zealand's significant art museums.

Dunedin Public Art Gallery

Collection: The gallery houses a fine collection of European art, New Zealand art from 1860 to the present, and significant holdings of Japanese prints and the decorative arts.
Exhibition schedule: Refer to the gallery website for current and future exhibitions.
Artists represented: Rita Angus, Sir Edward Burne-Jones, John Constable, Stanhope Forbes, Charles F. Goldie, Bill Hammond, Ando Hiroshige, Frances Hodgkins, Katsushika Hokusai, Claude Lorrain, Zanobi Machiavelli, Colin McCahon, Claude Monet, Michael Parekowhai, Charles Edward Perugini, Lucien Pissarro, Joshua Reynolds, Peter Robinson, Salvator Rosa, Stanley Spencer, Titian, Jacques-Joseph Tissot, Petrus van der Velden, Gordon Walters, Sir Toss Woollaston.
Where to eat: The award-winning Nova Café is situated in the gallery.
What else to do nearby: Browse in the well-stocked gallery shop; visit Dunedin's Botanic Garden and Chinese Garden and the Otago Settlers Museum; get active on the walking and mountain biking tracks.

Gallery De Novo (D)

Address: 101 Stuart Street, Dunedin
Phone number: (03) 474 9200
Website: www.gallerydenovo.co.nz
Gallery Directors: Elizabeth Fraser and Richelle Byers
Opening times: 9.30 am to 5.30 pm Monday to Friday; 10 am to 3 pm Saturday and Sunday.
Admission charges: Free
Guided tours: On request
Wheelchair access: Yes, into main gallery on street level.
Toilets: Yes

This popular Dunedin gallery is in a good central location midway between the Octagon and Dunedin Railway Station. It hosts a large collection of contemporary New Zealand art, including printmaking, paintings, sculpture, photography and jewellery. Gallery De Novo has a rotating exhibition schedule and a vast selection of stock artists shown between exhibitions. A global shipping service is available and there is an on-site framing workshop for customer framing consultations. The gallery also offers a local delivery and hanging service for artworks.

Collection: Sole representative of Suzy Platt paintings and prints. Exclusive New Zealand representatives of English-based artist Geoffrey Robinson, and the largest collection of Kelvin Mann etchings in New Zealand.

Exhibition schedule: Monthly exhibitions with mixed artists displayed in between.

Artists represented: Peter Beadle, Angela Burns, Lee Byford, Brian Dahlberg, Nic Dempster, Janet de Wagt, Ricky Drew, Kylie Duncan, Phillip Edwards, Frank Gordon, Shane Hansen, Ivan Hill, Maria Kemp, Kelvin Mann, Philip Maxwell, Ewan McDougall, Brad Novak, Suzy Platt, Geoffrey Robinson, Michael Smither, Mahiriki Tangaroa, Lynn Taylor, Marilynn Webb, Ben Webb, Weston Frizzell.

Where to eat: There are numerous cafés and restaurants nearby.

What else to do nearby: Visit Dunedin Public Art Gallery, Botanic and Chinese Gardens, City Library and Railway Station; tour Cadbury World at the Cadbury chocolate factory.

Gallery Thirty Three (D)

Address: *33 Helwick Street, Wanaka*
Phone number: *(03) 443 4330*
Website: *www.gallery33.co.nz*
Gallery Directors: *Peter Gregg and Norma Dutton, Melissa C. Reimer (Manager)*
Opening times: *10 am to 5.30 pm Monday* *to Friday; 10 am to 5 pm Saturday and Sunday.*
Admission charges: *Free*
Guided tours: *No, but private viewings are available on request.*
Wheelchair access: *Yes*
Toilets: *Public toilets nearby, within 50 metres.*

Wanaka's only contemporary art gallery. Gallery Thirty Three is a small and vibrant gallery exhibiting stunningly designed, often sculptural, jewellery and contemporary artwork in a range of media from favourite New Zealand artists. This gallery stocks unframed and framed works on paper, oils on linen and canvas, and small- and medium-scale sculptures in stone, bronze, glass, tin and other media. There is an excellent selection of small- and medium-scale cast glass works and small-scale, hand-blown glass works, as well as works in lead crystal. They also specialise in ceramics, both classic and quirky.

Gallery Thirty Three

Collection: The gallery does not have a permanent collection.
Exhibition schedule: Exhibitions preview on the first Friday of each month and also include guest artists. Preview is from 5 pm and all are welcome to enjoy a glass of wine and to meet the artist(s). Refer to the gallery website for current and future exhibitions.
Artists represented: Richard Adams, Don Binney, Katie Brown, Emma Camden, Madeleine Child and Philip Jarvis, Barry Clarke, Bing Dawe, Paul Dibble, Scott Eady, Jason Greig, Simon Kaan, Lukeke, Peter Miller, David Murray, J. S. Parker, Ben Reid, Annie Smits Sandano, Ian Scott, Amanda Shanley, Michael Smither, Llew Summers, Jenny Smith, Katie Thomas, Michel Tuffery.
Where to eat: The Federal Diner just down the road at 47 Helwick Street.
What else to do nearby: Lake Wanaka and its environs is the area's real drawcard. Gallery Thirty Three is the icing on the cake. Enjoy mountain biking, hiking, walking, swimming and dining.

Hullabaloo Art Space (A)

Address: *Melmore Terrace, Old Cromwell Historic Precinct, Cromwell*
Phone number: *027 600 7106*
Website: *www.hullabalooart.co.nz*
Gallery Director: *Odelle Morshuis*
Building: *The old Cromwell Bakery*

Opening times: *10 am to 4 pm daily.*
Admission charges: *Free*
Guided tours: *By appointment*
Wheelchair access: *Yes*
Toilets: *Yes*

Hullabaloo Art Space is a contemporary gallery with a collective of 14 artists from Central Otago and Dunedin. Included are painters, ceramicists, photographers and sculptors. The gallery is a spacious white-walled space with a continuing selection of pleasing creations. It is an artist-run initiative and as such an artist is always on duty to welcome visitors and advise on artworks.

Collection: The gallery does not have a permanent collection.
Exhibition schedule: Every 3 weeks a new solo show is hung and the gallery is changed once a month.
Artists represented: Odelle Morshuis, Rachel Hirabayashi, Nigel Wilson, Lynne Wilson, Liz Kempthorne, Liz Rowe, Sue Rutherford, Gail de Jong, Jillian Porteous, Eric Schusser, Annemarie Hope-Cross, Luke Anthony, Kay Todd, Andi Regan.
Where to eat: The lovely Grain and Seed Café is next door.
What else to do nearby: Wander around the historic precinct, which consists of many old schist buildings containing a variety of shops.

Joanne Deaker Fine Art Studio (A)

Address: 29 Coleraine Street, Cromwell
Phone number: (03) 445 3368 or 027 248 6116
Website: www.joannedeaker.co.nz
Gallery Director: Joanne Deaker
Building: Private residence

Opening times: By appointment only
Admission charges: Free
Guided tours: No
Wheelchair access: No
Toilets: No

Joanne Deaker has a small studio/gallery in the historic village of Cromwell where visitors have the opportunity to interact directly with the artist. Having given up a promising career as a veterinarian and animal scientist to pursue a career as an artist, it is no surprise her paintings have a rural theme. Joanne works with acrylics in a contemporary semi-impressionistic style often using a limited palette of three or four colours and lots of texture. Her paintings are exhibited in galleries nationwide and are held in both private and corporate collections internationally.

Collection: Joanne Deaker
Exhibition schedule: Variable, but paintings change at least every 2 months as they are sold or sent to other galleries or exhibitions.
Artist represented: Joanne Deaker
Where to eat: Nearby in the centre of town there is a variety of cafés and restaurants.
What else to do nearby: Visit the region's wineries and other studios and galleries; go walking or cycling in the area.

Metalworks Wanaka (A)

Address: 54 Ballantyne Road, Wanaka
Phone number: (03) 443 1760
Website: www.metalworkswanaka.co.nz
Gallery Directors: Ernie Maluschnig and Lizzi Yates
Building: Industrial workshop
Opening times: 9 am to 5 pm Monday to

Friday; Saturday and Sunday by appointment.
Admission charges: Free
Guided tours: The artist is in the workshop most days.
Wheelchair access: Able to provide a ramp if advised prior to visit.
Toilets: No

You will find this intimate gallery space in an industrial workshop of Metalworks Wanaka, established in 1997 by Ernie Maluschnig. It showcases the art and sculpture of Ernie, together with some special pieces from the Metalworks workshop. Metalworks Wanaka is a business known for creative fine design and craftsmanship. There are always creative happenings in the workshop, which is accessible and visible from the gallery.

Collection: Stainless and metal sculpture. Exhibited nationally: *Midnight, Vanishing Point, Tailing, Sluicing, Slice of Heaven, Relief 202, Stainless Sails, Aspire, Rusty Sails, Ground Relief, Unfolding.*

Exhibition schedule: The gallery does not have a regular exhibition schedule.
Artists represented: Ernie Maluschnig
Where to eat: There are cafés and restaurants 1.5 kilometres away in Wanaka township.
What else to do nearby: Visit other galleries in town; sample fine wines; walk in pristine environment.

Milford Galleries Dunedin (D)

Address: 18 Dowling Street, Dunedin
Phone number: (03) 477 7727
Website: www.milfordgalleries.co.nz
Gallery Directors: Stephen Higginson and Niki Stewart
Building: The gallery is in an historic building built in 1883. It was home to the New Zealand Clothing Factory warehouse and was the headquarters for the Hallenstein Brothers New Zealand Clothing Factory until 1988.
Opening times: 9 am to 5.30 pm Monday to Friday; 11 am to 3 pm Saturday, or by appointment.
Admission charges: Free
Guided tours: No
Wheelchair access: No
Toilets: Public toilets nearby in the Dunedin City Council Dowling Street car park.

Milford Galleries Dunedin is located in the heart of Dunedin. The gallery consists of three main spaces – two large rooms and a smaller more intimate space. One of the gallery's distinctive features is that irrespective of the solo exhibition programme there is always a large variety of work available to view. Milford Galleries Dunedin presents exhibitions that report the quality and diversity of New Zealand art and the gallery seeks to support and contribute to the dialogue between national and international artists and their audiences. The gallery features solo and group exhibitions of New Zealand art, including painting, sculpture, glass, ceramics, photography and works on paper. Catalogues of the gallery's full holdings are available for visitors to browse through at leisure and all work is held on-site in one of New Zealand's largest art storerooms.

Milford Galleries Dunedin

Collection: The gallery does not have a permanent collection.
Exhibition schedule: The gallery combines a programme of solo and group exhibitions of new work by its exhibiting artists with selected works from the secondary market. A new exhibition is opened every 4 weeks.
Artists represented: Galia Amsel, Wayne Barrar, Graham Bennett, Marc Blake, Joanna Braithwaite, Nigel Brown, Simon Clark, Garry Currin, Niki Hastings-McFall, Michael Hight, Hannah Kidd, Peata Larkin, Karl Maughan, Geoffrey Notman, Richard Orjis, Reuben Paterson, Lorraine Rastorfer, Ann Robinson, Christine Thacker, Gary Waldrom.
Where to eat: Try the café Eat or The Palms Restaurant.
What else to do nearby: Visit Dunedin Public Art Gallery, Botanic and Chinese Gardens, or Railway Station, and the Otago Early Settlers Museum.

Milford Galleries Queenstown (D)

Address: 9A Earl Street, Queenstown
Phone number: (03) 442 6896
Website: www.milfordgalleries.co.nz
Gallery Directors: Stephen Higginson and
  Niki Stewart, Maurice Watson (Manager)
Opening times: 10 am to 6 pm daily, or by
appointment.
Admission charges: Free
Guided tours: No
Wheelchair access: Yes
Toilets: Public toilets nearby on the waterfront
at the end of Earl Street.

Milford Galleries Queenstown exhibits paintings and a variety of other fine art media drawn from the studios of many significant New Zealand contemporary artists. The main downstairs gallery allows for the installation of a large number of works while maintaining an intimate gallery experience. The upstairs gallery presents solo exhibitions and holds the gallery's storeroom, which contains a large number of works. Catalogues of the full holdings are available for visitors to browse.

Milford Galleries Queenstown

Collection: The gallery does not have a permanent collection.
Exhibition schedule: Exhibitions combine a programme of new work by exhibiting artists with curated exhibitions of selected works from the secondary market.
Artists represented: Callum Arnold, Tony Bishop, Claudia Borella, Christine Cathie, Evelyn Dunstan, John Edgar, Simon Edwards, Dick Frizzell, Stanley Palmer, Reuben Paterson, Sue Hawker, Megan Huffadine, Bruce Hunt, Luke Jacomb, Neal Palmer, John Parker, Mike Petre, Elizabeth Rees, Emily Siddell, Peter James Smith, Terry Stringer.
Where to eat: Try Botswana Butchery, Wai Waterfront Restaurant, Joe's Garage, or Halo.
What else to do nearby: Visit other galleries, Queenstown Botanical Gardens; take a ride on the Kawarau Jet Boats; tour Lake Wakatipu on the historic TSS *Earnslaw* steamship; for amazing views ride the Skyline Gondola.

Moray Gallery (D)

Address: 55 Princes Street, Dunedin
Phone number: (03) 477 8060
Website: www.moraygallery.com
Gallery Director: Jennifer Hopkinson
Building: Centrally located in central Dunedin close to the Octagon.
Opening times: 10 am to 5 pm Monday to Friday; 11 am to 3 pm Saturday.
Admission charges: Free
Guided tours: No
Wheelchair access: Yes
Toilets: Public toilets near Dunedin Town Hall, about 400 metres away.

Moray Gallery is a boutique art gallery situated close to the Dunedin Public Art Gallery in the centre of the city. The gallery features paintings in oil, acrylic and watercolour from local and South Island artists, plus a wide selection of artist prints both framed and unframed. The gallery currently holds the largest selection of watercolours by the late Annie Baird. Complementary to the paintings the gallery displays a fine selection of original blown and cast glass made by New Zealand's finest glass artists, as well as studio ceramics created by reputable local potters. Well-known Dunedin printmakers also feature strongly in this gallery. In-home art consultancy and art valuation services are offered and packaging and international posting services are available.

Collection: The gallery does not have a permanent collection.
Exhibition schedule: Refer to the gallery website for current and future exhibitions.
Artists represented: Jo Ogier, Gillian Pope, John Z. Robinson, Mary E. Taylor, Cynthia Taylor, Penny Smith, Nigel Wilson, Pat Corballis, Pia Davie, Riki Julin, Danny Moorwood, Garry Nash, Peter Viesnik, Shona Firman, Keith Mahy, John Penman, Peter Collis, Steve Fulmer, Ron van der Vlugt, Yi-Ming Lin.
Where to eat: A variety of cafés and restaurants can be found nearby.
What else to do nearby: Visit Dunedin Public Art Gallery and Larnach Castle and Gardens, only a 20-minute drive away.

Nadene Milne Gallery (D)

Address: *16 Buckingham Street, Arrowtown*
Phone number: *(03) 442 0467*
Website: *www.nadenemilnegallery.com*
Gallery Director: *Nadene Milne*
Building: *Historic 1860s Arrowtown building down 'one of New Zealand's most interesting alleyways'.*

Opening times: *10 am to 5 pm Saturday and Sunday; Monday to Friday by appointment.*
Admission charges: *Free*
Guided tours: *No*
Wheelchair access: *No*
Toilets: *Yes*

Nadene Milne Gallery is a high-end contemporary gallery that showcases many of New Zealand's most influential artists. Over the past 10 years, Nadene Milne has developed an excellent reputation for her quality exhibitions and continuing support of established New Zealand artists. A distinguishing feature of this gallery is the ongoing lecture series. Many exhibitions are supported with a lecture presentation given by the artist, or an associated curator or scholar, and held in the adjacent Dorothy Browns Cinema. The lectures help contextualise the practice of each artist and, it is hoped, help the audience understand the role contemporary art plays in the modern world.

Collection: As well as representing many of the country's greatest artists, the gallery also exhibits work by major artists such as Colin McCahon, Gordon Walters, Ralph Hotere, Shane Cotton and Michael Parekowhai.
Exhibition schedule: A monthly exhibition schedule including solo shows by represented artists as well as curated group shows featuring works of significance from the stockroom.
Artists represented: Rohan Wealleans, Ans Westra, Russell Moses, Neil Pardington, Max Gimblett, Heather Straka, Gretchen Albrecht, Elizabeth Thomson, Fiona Pardington, Peter Peryer, Tony Lane.
Where to eat: The award-winning Saffron Restaurant is next door.
What else to do nearby: Watch a film at Dorothy Browns Cinema; enjoy an abundance of magnificent scenic walking trails; pan for gold in the Arrow River; try the excellent cafés and restaurants; browse the eclectic mix of shops nearby.

Russell Henderson Art Gallery (D)

Address: *21 Centennial Avenue, Alexandra*
Phone number: *(03) 448 6230*
Website: *www.centralstories.com*
Gallery Director: *Brian Patrick*
Building: *Purpose-built, 77 square metre gallery constructed in Central Otago schist*
Opening times: *9 am to 6 pm (summer:*

Labour Weekend to Easter Weekend inclusive); 9 am to 5 pm (winter). Closed Christmas Day.
Admission charges: *Free, donations welcome.*
Guided tours: *Occasional artist's floor talks; contact the gallery for upcoming events.*
Wheelchair access: *Yes, wheelchair available for use.*
Toilets: *Yes*

The Russell Henderson Art Gallery was established in the Central Stories Museum and Art Gallery complex in December 2005. Exhibitions celebrate local artists as well as a selection from outside the Central Otago area. Artworks in a range of mediums are welcome and can be exhibited concurrently.

Collection: Central Stories Museum and Art Gallery has a permanent collection featuring a large collection of Elizabeth Stevens' paintings.

Exhibition schedule: The gallery generally has a 6-week rotation of exhibitions.

Artists represented: Past exhibitions have included artists such as Janet de Wagt, Sue Noble-Adams, Barrie Wills, Vivian McLatchie, Cynthia Miller, Susie Ruddenklau, Sharon Gilchrist, Central Otago Art Society, Rebecca Gilmore, Olwynne Oliver, Alan Waters, John Douglas, Gilbert van Reenen, Russell Shaw, Alastair Begg, Maxine Williams, Peter Peryer, Deidre Copeland, Pauline Bellamy, Hullabaloo Collective, Greg McDonald, Elissa Ramsay, Marg Hamilton, Manu Berry, Rachel Hirabayashi.

Where to eat: The Tin Goose opposite the Central Stories building has delicious coffee and café food. Monteith's Brewery Bar offers bistro food and beverages.

What else to do nearby: The Alexandra Visitor Information Centre is located in the Central Stories building. A walking tour of the town visits key historic buildings, Flat Top Hill Conservation Area and the Earnscleugh Tailings Reserve. Explore the mighty Clutha River and isolated reaches of the historic picturesque Roxburgh Gorge with Clutha River Cruises.

The Artists Room Gallery (D)

Address: *Level 1, 2 Dowling Street, Dunedin*
Phone number: *(03) 474 1111*
Website: *www.theartistsroom.co.nz*
Gallery Director: *Michelle Chalklin-Sinclair*
Building: *Historic Commerce Building on the corner of Dowling and Burlington Streets.*
Opening times: *10 am to 5 pm Monday to Friday; 12 pm to 2 pm Saturday, or by appointment.*
Admission charges: *Free*
Guided tours: *No*
Wheelchair access: *No*
Toilets: *No*

This gallery is situated on the first and second floors of one of Dunedin's historic buildings and overlooks the beautiful Queens Gardens. It is located in the heart of the Dowling Street arts quarter. The Artists Room Gallery represents some of New Zealand's top artists in all mediums – painting, printmaking, sculpture and photography. The gallery also has an art restoration service and is a guild-commended framer.

Collection: The gallery does not have a permanent collection.

Exhibition schedule: A revolving exhibition schedule with one to two exhibitions held each month featuring a variety of New Zealand artists.

Artists represented: Michel Tuffery, Colin Wheeler, Jenny Dolezel, Sam Foley, Donna Demente, Stephen Martyn Welch, John Badcock, Tony Cribb, Crispin Korschen, Llew Summers, Cheryl Oliver, Helen Back, Sue Syme, Anya Sinclair, Kate Alterio, Claire Beynon,

Manu Berry, Olav Nielsen, Steev Peyroux, Robyn Kahukiwa, Peter Cleverly, Geoff Williams, Inge Doesburg, Greg Lewis.
Where to eat: There are numerous local cafés and restaurants.
What else to do nearby: Visit Dunedin Public Art Gallery, Botanic and Chinese Gardens; tour Cadbury World at the Cadbury chocolate factory or take in Speight's Brewery.

Toi o Tahuna (D)

Address: 11 Church Lane, Queenstown
Phone number: (03) 409 0787
Website: www.toi.co.nz
Gallery Director: Mark Moran,
Andrew Jeffery (Manager)
Building: The gallery is situated in the same
building as RadioNetwork.
Opening times: 10 am to 6 pm daily.
Admission charges: Free
Guided tours: On request
Wheelchair access: Yes
Toilets: Yes

The gallery is located in Queenstown and showcases emerging and established contemporary Maori artists from Aotearoa New Zealand. There is a wide selection of paintings, sculpture, limited edition prints and photographs.

Collection: Estate of John Bevan Ford
Exhibition schedule: The gallery holds up to six individual or group shows a year.
Artists represented: Roi Toia, Todd Couper, David Teata, Aaron Kereopa, Tracey Tawhiao, Rangi Kipa, Sofia Minson, Jenufa Waiti, Robyn Kahukiwa, Manos Nathan, Luke Leaf.
Where to eat: Try Les Alpes Restaurant or No. 5 Church Lane Bar & Restaurant at The Spire Hotel.
What else to do nearby: The possibilities are endless in and around Queenstown: art trails, sightseeing, walking, adventure tourism, scenic flights, wine tours, horse trekking, golf, skiing in winter and much more.

Whisky Art Gallery (D)

Address: 14–16 Harbour Street, Oamaru
Phone number: 022 437 0789
Website: www.whiskyartgallery.com
Gallery Directors: Dawn Mann and Kathryn Mann
Building: The Loan and Mercantile Building is New Zealand's most significant 19th-century industrial building. It has a New Zealand Historic Places Trust Category I listing. Built in 1882, to the design of Dennison and Grant, this elegantly detailed three-storey
Victorian warehouse was built for New Zealand Loan and Mercantile when it was the largest stock and station agency in New Zealand.
Opening times: 11 am to 4 pm daily (summer), or by appointment.
Admission charges: Free
Guided tours: No
Wheelchair access: No
Toilets: Yes, available if requested.

Whisky Art Gallery is on the top floor of the historic New Zealand Loan and Mercantile Building in the old quarter of Oamaru. The gallery features paintings by South Island artists in watercolour, oil and pastel, and sculptures by Otago artist Mike Assie.

Collection: Whilst this gallery does not have a permanent collection of art, the floor beneath the gallery houses hundreds of barrels of maturing whisky, adding to the gallery's unique aroma of whisky, sea breezes and aged building.
Exhibition schedule: Artists are permanently represented in their own areas in the gallery.
Artists represented: Dawn Mann, Kit MacGregor, Pauline Bellamy, Manu Berry, Chris Wilkie, Ewan McDougall, Mike Glover, Alison Bevers, Dave Thomas, Chris Muldrew.
Where to eat: The Loan and Merc Eating House and Tavern (Fleur's Other Place) is on the ground floor (Fleur Sullivan from Fleur's Place opened this second restaurant recently).
What else to do nearby: Oamaru's historic precinct remains one of New Zealand's most complete Victorian streetscapes. Walk around the many original 19th-century stone buildings.

Wilson Gallery (A)

Address: 45 Beach Street, Queenstown
Phone number: (03) 441 2490
Website: www.timwilsonart.com
Gallery Director: Arju Ekanayake
Building: The Mountaineer Building
Opening times: 11 am to 4 pm and 7.30 pm to 10 pm Tuesday to Sunday (summer); 12 pm to 5 pm Monday, Tuesday, Thursday, Saturday (winter).
Admission charges: Free
Guided tours: No
Wheelchair access: Yes
Toilets: No

Visiting Wilson Gallery in the historic Mountaineer Building with its elegant Georgian architecture and understated interior ambience is an experience in itself. Wilson Gallery is the exclusive representative of the extraordinary and unique works of New Zealand's premier landscape painter Tim Wilson. His finely detailed work can be found in galleries and homes around the world. Trained as a jeweller, and without formal education in art, he paints real mountains, lakes and skies using as many as 30 layers of transparent glazes and interference pigments to achieve the mesmerizing play of light in his work which captures the unique beauty and spirit of New Zealand's landscape. The gallery features fellow Kiwi artist Anita May Blanchett, a master of high realism, guest artists and exhibitions in the heart of Queenstown.

Collection: Tim Wilson, Anita May Blanchett
Exhibition schedule: Contact the gallery for a schedule of current and future exhibitions.
Artists represented: Tim Wilson, Anita May Blanchett
Where to eat: There are many quality cafés, restaurants and bars in the area.
What else to do nearby: The sky is the limit. Gondola rides, trip on the lake, spa, upmarket clothing stores, lakefront walk, restaurants and bars, numerous sightseeing options.

Southland

Anderson Park Art Gallery (P)

Address: 91 McIvor Road, RD 6,
Waikiwi, Invercargill
Phone number: (03) 215 7432
Website: The gallery does not have a website.
Gallery Director: Helen Nicoll
Building: New Zealand Historic Places
Trust Category 1 listed building

Opening times: 10.30 am to 5 pm daily.
Closed Good Friday and Christmas Day.
Admission charges: Voluntary donation
Guided tours: On request
Wheelchair access: Yes
Toilets: Yes

This neo-Georgian historic house is set in 24 hectares of landscaped gardens and is home to an extensive collection of New Zealand art. There are beautiful original antique furnishings, block prints, pottery, sculptures, grand landscapes, Greek-mythic Maori village scenes and portraits. The generous gardens are a lovely place to linger, with trees and trails, a children's playground and a wharepuni (sleeping house).

Collection: Over 1000 works in the collection featuring prominent New Zealand artists from late 19th century to the present day.
Exhibition schedule: The Annual Spring Exhibition is held every October.
Artists represented: Artists from throughout New Zealand. All works for sale.
Where to eat: Complimentary tea and coffee provided, or visit Café Greenworld Lynwood Homestead (200 North Road).
What else to do nearby: Visit Queens Park, Southland Museum and Art Gallery and the city centre. It is a 30-minute drive to Bluff, Riverton or Winton.

ArtSouth Gallery of Fine Art (D)

Address: 101 Main Street, Gore
Phone number: (03) 208 0001
Website: www.artsouth.co.nz
Gallery Director: Bob Martin
Building: Historic, 100-year-old red brick building
formerly the Post Office and Telephone Exchange.

Opening times: 11 am to 3 pm Tuesday to
Friday; 11 am to 1 pm Saturday.
Admission charges: Free
Guided tours: By appointment
Wheelchair access: No
Toilets: No

Occupying the upper level of a 100-year-old historic red brick building (formerly the original Post Office and Telephone Exchange), this gallery always displays a diverse range of original, contemporary, historic, modern and traditional work from local, national and international artists. Quality, hand-blown glass, ceramics, prints and cards are also available. There are five display galleries including the Miniatures Room (the first telephone booth in Gore) and Alveridgea Gallery, which features Ivan Clarke's Lonely Dog Editions of prints, bronzes and books. Watch out for the upcoming Warner Bros movie of the Lonely Dog story as announced in 2009, and the worldwide publication *Alveridgea: The Legend of the Lonely Dog* (2011) in bookshops. This is just one of a number of artists represented by ArtSouth who are making history at the very highest levels on the international art scene.

Collection: Doris Lusk, Alan Pearson, Wallace Keown (exclusive sales), Lonely Dog Editions (exclusive representation), Makoure Scott – *Aotearoa Space Abstractions Series #1* (part of the Deep Space Art Collection; exclusive New Zealand representation).
Exhibition schedule: Refer to the gallery website for current and future exhibitions.
Artists represented: Pauline Bellamy, Graham Brinsley, Liz Bristow, Paul Cato, Beverly Claridge, Ivan Clarke, Shirley Cleary, Judith Lane Ewing, Fiona Goulding, Julie Greig, Robert John Martin, Keith Morant, Naked Art, Rosemary Parcell, Nathaneal Provis, Makoure Scott, Ashley Shaw, Brian Strong, Tony Tarasievicz, Mackenzie Thorpe, Barry Weston, Nigel Wilson, Claire Worrall, Emma Wright.
Where to eat: Old Post Bakery Café is on the ground floor.
What else to do nearby: Visit Eastern Southland Gallery, Hokonui Moonshine Museum, Gore Airforce Museum, Gore Historical Museum and the Croydon Aircraft and Steam Locomotive Museum, Manderville Aerodrome.

Eastern Southland Museum

Eastern Southland Museum (P)

Address: Cnr Hokonui Drive and
Norfolk Street, Gore
Phone number: (03) 208 9907
Website: The gallery does not have a website.
District Curator: Jim Geddes
Building: Formerly Carnegie Library built in
1909. It was one of 18 libraries funded by
American philanthropist Andrew Carnegie
in New Zealand.
Opening times: 10 am to 4.30 pm Monday to
Friday; 1 pm to 4 pm Saturday and Sunday,
and some public holidays. Closed Good
Friday, Christmas Day, Boxing Day and New
Year's Day.
Admission charges: Free, donations
welcome.
Guided tours: By appointment
Wheelchair access: Yes
Toilets: Yes

Nicknamed the 'Goreggenheim' by Saatchi & Saatchi boss Kevin Roberts, the Eastern
Southland Gallery is a regional public art museum, situated in the Arts and Heritage Precinct
in Gore's city centre. Established in a former Carnegie Library building, it features permanent
exhibitions dedicated to the collection of expatriate New Zealander Dr John Money and
the works of major New Zealand artist Ralph Hotere. It also has a vibrant programme of
temporary exhibitions, performances, workshops and artist projects.

Collection: Permanent displays include significant works by Bambarra, Baga and Dogon
carvers of West Africa, major works by New Zealand artists Rita Angus, Theo Schoon and
Ralph Hotere, and paintings by Australian and American artists including the New York-based
artist Lowell Nesbitt.
Exhibition schedule: Two permanent exhibitions – the Dr John Money Collection and
Ralph Hotere Collection. Regular temporary exhibitions, performances, workshops and artist
projects are held in two dedicated gallery spaces.
Artists represented: As above
Where to eat: There are cafés and restaurants in central Gore.
What else to do nearby: Visit Hokonui Moonshine Museum, Gore Airforce Museum,
Gore Historical Museum, and the Croydon Aircraft and Steam Locomotive Museum,
Mandeville Aerodrome.

Southland Museum and Art Gallery (Niho o Te Taniwha) (P)

Address: 108 Gala Street, Invercargill
Phone number: (03) 219 9069
Website: www.southlandmuseum.com
Gallery Director: Gael Ramsay
Opening times: 9 am to 5 pm Monday to
Friday; 10 am to 5 pm Saturday, Sunday and
public holidays. Closed Christmas Day.
Admission charges: Donation
Guided tours: Yes, bookings required for
larger groups.
Wheelchair access: Yes
Toilets: Yes

Southland Museum and Art Gallery consists of four galleries with exhibitions selected to provide a balanced variety from all sectors of the arts. The community access gallery highlights work by local artists; galleries two, three and four feature exhibitions from around New Zealand.

Collection: Contact the gallery for information on the collection.
Exhibition schedule: Refer to the gallery website for current and future exhibitions.
Artists represented: Wide selection of New Zealand artists.
Where to eat: Artworks Café is located in the museum.
What else to do nearby: Explore Queens Park with its gardens, statues, playground, golf course and tearooms.

Southland Museum and Art Gallery

Index